RAND

The Public Benefit of Energy Efficiency to the State of Minnesota

Mark Bernstein, Christopher Pernin, Sam Loeb, Mark Hanson

Prepared for the
Energy Foundation

RAND Science and Technology

The research described in this report was conducted by RAND Science and Technology for the Energy Foundation.

Library of Congress Cataloging-in-Publication Data

The public benefit of energy efficiency to the state of Minnesota / Mark Bernstein ... [et al.].
    p. cm.
    "MR-1587."
    Includes bibliographical referencesm and index.
    ISBN 0-8330-3196-1
    1. Energy policy—Economic aspects—Minnesota. 2. Energy conservation—Economic aspects—Minnesota. I. Bernstein, Mark, 1956–

HD9502.U53 M658 2002
333.79'17'09776—dc21

2002067972

RAND is a nonprofit institution that helps improve policy and decisionmaking through research and analysis. RAND® is a registered trademark. RAND's publications do not necessarily reflect the opinions or policies of its research sponsors.

Published 2002 by RAND
1700 Main Street, P.O. Box 2138, Santa Monica, CA 90407-2138
1200 South Hayes Street, Arlington, VA 22202-5050
201 North Craig Street, Suite 202, Pittsburgh, PA 15213-1516
RAND URL: http://www.rand.org/
To order RAND documents or to obtain additional information, contact Distribution Services: Telephone: (310) 451-7002; Fax: (310) 451-6915; Email: order@rand.org

Preface

This report assesses the benefits of energy efficiency to the Minnesota state economy, its environment, and its citizens. Energy efficiency and its effects are difficult to measure directly. This analysis estimates energy efficiency through its effects on energy consumption and economic productivity (i.e., a form of energy intensity—the energy consumed per unit of output) while controlling for price, sectoral composition, and other factors. Furthermore, this study is limited to improvements in the use of energy in the industrial, commercial, and residential sectors and does not include, for example, the transportation sector. Conceivably, improvements in energy usage in the industrial, commercial, and residential sectors could yield a number of benefits, including economic gains, improved productivity, improved quality of service, higher reliability, reduced pollution, and lower costs to consumers. This report addresses three of these benefits:

- Effects on the gross state product of energy efficiency improvements in the commercial and industrial sectors.

- Effects on air emissions of the improved utilization of energy in the commercial and industrial sectors.

- Effects on households, particularly low-income households, of improvements in residential energy efficiency.

This study does not show causality between government investments in energy efficiency and reduced energy consumption although state audits have concluded they exist. Rather, this study is limited in its ability to directly compare energy efficiency programs to actual improvements in energy efficiency.

This study was funded by the Energy Foundation, a partnership of major foundations interested in sustainable energy. The results are intended to inform policymakers and the general public about the benefits of energy efficiency programs in Minnesota, to help these readers to understand the role of the government in promoting these programs, and to provide useful information for national and local policymakers when they consider funding for energy efficiency programs in the future.

The authors would like to thank those individuals and organizations who helped in the research and preparation of the report. A partial listing includes Steve Rakow, Phil Smith, and Mike Taylor at the Minnesota Department of Commerce; and RAND's internal and external reviewers of the report.

This research was performed by members of RAND Science and Technology. RAND is a nonprofit, nonpartisan research organization. For further information on this report, please contact Mark Bernstein (markb@rand.org).

Contents

Figures

Tables

Summary

RAND, a nonprofit and nonpartisan research organization, has prepared this report with funding from the Energy Foundation, a partnership of major foundations interested in sustainable energy.

In this study, we estimate energy efficiency from measures of energy intensity[1] that have been controlled for sectoral composition, energy prices, and other factors. In this report we address the public benefits of our estimate of energy efficiency to Minnesota and find that improvements in energy efficiency in the commercial, industrial, and residential sectors are associated with

- a benefit to the state economy since 1977 that ranges from $793 per capita to $903 per capita in 1998 dollars[2]
- approximately 18 percent lower air emissions from stationary sources
- a reduced energy burden on low-income households.

This study measures the benefit to the state economy of improvements in energy efficiency in the industrial and commercial sectors from 1977 to 1997. It also predicts the potential future impacts of continued improvements in energy efficiency.

There are four key issues and assumptions in this report:

- This analysis shows that declines in energy intensity (the energy consumed per unit of output) are associated with increases in GSP (gross state product) when sectoral composition, energy prices, and other factors are held constant.

- When these factors are held constant, changes in energy intensity can be an approximation of changes in energy efficiency. Thus, the conclusion is that improvements in energy efficiency are associated with improvements in gross state product.

---

[1] Energy intensity is commonly defined as energy use per unit of output. Energy efficiency is commonly accepted as either reducing the amount of energy for a given output or increasing the output for a given level of energy.

[2] Except where otherwise noted, economic variables are deflated according to the Producer Price Index for Finished Goods, with base year 1982, and expressed in 1998 dollars (1998$).

- Government investments in energy efficiency programs may lead to improvements in GSP. At this point, we do not know how government programs affect the overall energy efficiency as used in the GSP analysis.

- Estimates of the economic benefits of efficiency programs are compared with changes in GSP resulting from energy efficiency.

Effects on the Minnesota Economy

In this study, the GSP per capita is our indicator of economic performance. We use a conventional economic approach to measure the growth in GSP per capita, in which state economic growth is correlated with the stock and flow of capital and labor, with government policies, and with the characteristics of the population. The GSP measures the value of outputs from all economic sectors in the state. GSP per capita in Minnesota grew by more than 67 percent from 1977 to 1997. The growth in GSP is due to a variety of factors, including but not limited to the industrial composition of the state, the growth of industry output, the growth of commercial establishments, and demographic changes in the state.

We hypothesize that changes in energy intensity—the energy consumed per unit output—have also had an effect on the growth of GSP per capita. By controlling for various exogenous factors such as price, industrial mix, new capital, and climate, we attempt to capture changes in energy intensity associated with energy efficiency that have resulted partly from changes in government policies (e.g., financial support for energy efficiency programs.)[3]

Energy Efficiency in Minnesota: 1977–1997

The energy intensity of the industrial and commercial sectors in the state has declined considerably, although inconsistently, since 1977. Despite an increase in total energy consumption in Minnesota during that period, energy consumption per dollar of GSP has declined in both the industrial and commercial sectors. The contributing factors to these changes are many. Widespread use of new technologies and implementation of the state's building energy code may have supported, in part, the observed improvements in energy efficiency and declines in energy intensity. Increases in the price of energy from the late 1970s to the mid-1980s contributed to the declines in energy intensity as well. In addition, the

---

[3]However, establishing the causality between government energy efficiency programs and decreases in energy intensity as used in the economic growth analysis is beyond the scope of this project.

composition of the industrial sector changed over the period of study: The proportion of energy intensive manufacturing industries in the state declined in the mid- to late 1980s, and this reduced the aggregate amount of energy used per unit of output.

Our model includes controls for exogenous factors, such as the composition of industry and energy prices, to better isolate the changes in energy intensity associated with energy efficiency. Figure S.1 shows the growth of GSP per capita from 1977 to 1997 and the estimated growth of GSP per capita in the absence of independent improvements in energy intensity. Our model indicates that when controlling for those factors, if there had been no improvement in energy intensity from 1977 to 1997, the Minnesota economy would have been nearly 5 percent smaller than it was in 1997. In other words, the benefit in 1997 to the state economy from improvements in industrial and commercial energy intensity since 1979 ranges from $793 per capita to $903 per capita. The changes in energy intensity that are associated with economic growth in the state are those that are independent of the exogenous factors named above. These changes may be the effect of government policy in the form of energy efficiency programs. To draw a more solid conclusion, we need better data for national demand side management (DSM) expenditures. Absent this information, we take an indirect approach to evaluate these programs.

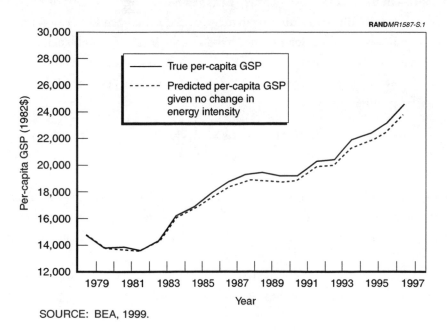

SOURCE: BEA, 1999.

Figure S.1—Actual GSP Per Capita from 1979 to 1997 in Minnesota and GSP Per Capita in the Case of Constant Energy Intensity

Between 1996 and 1999, Minnesota utilities invested $79.3 million in approximately 29,868 GWh of energy savings in the commercial and industrial sectors, at an average rate of $2,655/GWh. While annual investments in energy efficiency declined over that period from $24.1 million to $18.3 million, our model results show benefits to GSP of $9.7 billion, corresponding to 275,646 GWh of savings ($35,368/GWh) associated with decreased energy intensity during that period.

Energy Efficiency and the State Economy: 2000–2015

Population growth in Minnesota over the past 20 years has increased demand for new energy supplies and has inspired investment in conservation programs over that same period. While Minnesota has achieved significant benefits from reductions in energy intensity since the late 1970s, the future of energy use and energy efficiency programs in the state remains uncertain. Minnesota's total population is expected to increase by more than 7 percent over the next 15 years (MSDC, 1998). Population growth will be driven by the suburban counties in the Minneapolis/St. Paul metropolitan area. Minnesotans live in a severe climate region, where cooling and heating loads are greater; thus, businesses and residences located in these areas will continue to require higher energy intensities in the future. Lower energy prices in the long term, use of new electronic household and office appliances, and the increased energy load for space conditioning could lead to increased energy intensity in all sectors. The state's energy connection to other states, via the Mid-Continent Area Power Pool (MAPP) power grid, also connects the state to the region's potential demand and reliability problems as well.

After controlling for various factors, the analysis shows that reduced energy intensity is associated with economic growth. Energy intensity in the industrial and commercial sectors in Minnesota declined overall from 1977 to 1997. In the period from 1977 to 1987, energy intensity decreased in both commercial and industrial sectors, followed by an increase in industrial energy intensity from 1987 to 1997. Looking to the future, if energy intensity were to decline according to the 1977 to 1987 rate, GSP per capita in 2015 could be $1,026 higher than it would have been if energy intensity remained at its 1997 level. On the other hand, if energy intensity were to continue to decline at the overall 1977 to 1997 rate, the benefit to GSP in 2015 could be approximately $459 per capita. Thus, after controlling for various factors, we find that continued declines in energy intensity could continue to benefit the state economy. However, if energy intensity were to reverse the 1977 to 1997 trend, GSP per capita could drop approximately $456. Based on our economic methodology, any estimates of benefits of reduced energy intensity must be cautiously interpreted as upper bounds.

Environmental Benefits

One of many environmental benefits associated with improved energy efficiency is the effect on air emissions. In our analysis, we find that if energy intensity in the state had remained at 1977 levels, air emissions as a result of power consumption could be approximately 18 percent greater than current levels. These changes are felt throughout the MAPP because Minnesota purchases its power from a variety of sources in the region. While motor vehicles are the primary contributors to air emissions and the transportation sector has grown dramatically over the past 20 years, reductions in energy intensity in the commercial and industrial sectors have allowed Minnesota to slow the growth of emissions despite increases in energy consumption throughout the state (see Figure S.2).

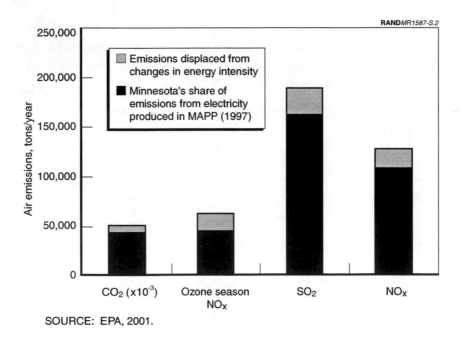

SOURCE: EPA, 2001.

Figure S.2—Emission Reductions in Minnesota

Benefits to the Citizens

Unlike energy intensity and GSP in the industrial and commercial sector, there is no easily quantifiable parameter with which to evaluate the benefits of energy efficiency to the residential sector. Furthermore, statewide economic benefits of reduced energy consumption in the residential sector are uncertain: Modest increases in disposable income may not manifest themselves as large-scale economic benefits to the state. It is clear, however, that investments in energy efficiency do reduce household energy costs and that these investments are cost-effective. In Minnesota, the average energy expenditures per capita in real terms has decreased from $718 in 1982 to $477 in 1992. This decline is due both to changes in energy use per household and real energy prices. These are real economic benefits to Minnesota residents.

Energy efficiency has the potential to reduce household energy costs across all income levels (see Figure S.3), but low-income households derive the greatest benefit from reduced energy expenditures. While low-income households spend less on energy than higher income households, the burden as a percentage of income is higher for lower-income populations. Thus, reduced energy costs in lower-income households increase disposable income at a higher rate than in higher-income households.

On average, low-income households nationwide spend 8 percent of their income on electricity, compared with 2 percent of a median-income household. In very poor households—those below 50 percent of the federal poverty level—23 percent of household income may be spent on electricity. A 1993 survey found that low-income households spend more for water heating than median income

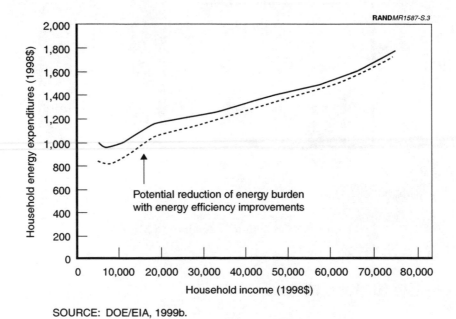

SOURCE: DOE/EIA, 1999b.

Figure S.3—Minnesota Household Energy Expenditures

households and spend almost as much on space heating, even though low-income homes are 40 percent smaller in size. Most of the energy-related services provided to these households are low quality, using inefficient appliances and inadequate heating and cooling.

The opportunities for energy efficiency in households can provide direct benefits for low-income consumers. Energy efficiency programs at the household level provide two services: (1) they directly reduce monthly energy costs, thereby increasing the disposable income (after energy costs are paid) of the population (and consequently increase the disposable income of the low-income population by a greater percentage than high-income households), and (2) they improve quality of life by improving the comfort level in homes.

Federal Low-Income Home Energy Assistance Program (LIHEAP) allocations have declined by more than one-half since the mid-1980s and do not fully serve the targeted, low-income population. In Minnesota, LIHEAP served only 25 percent of the eligible population in the late 1990s (NCAT, 2001a, 2001b). In 1997, Minnesota was allotted $37.5 million and also received $13.7 million in emergency funds that year (DHHS, 2001). More recent energy price shocks have created new political support for LIHEAP funding—with 2001 allotments of $54.4 million and emergency funds of $34.8 million to Minnesota (NCAT, 2001a, 2001b).

Conclusions

Declines in energy intensity are strongly associated with increased economic growth, improved air quality, and direct benefits to Minnesota residents. Conversely, future increases in energy intensity could reverse these trends. While these declines have coincided with investments in energy efficiency, we have not specifically evaluated the link between energy efficiency programs and improvements in energy intensity.

Acronyms

ACEEE	American Council for an Energy Efficient Economy
Btu	British Thermal Unit
CO_2	Carbon Dioxide
CO	Carbon Monoxide
CPI	Consumer Price Index
DHHS	U.S. Department of Health and Human Services
DOE	U.S. Department of Energy
DSM	Demand Side Management
EIA	U.S. Department of Energy, Energy Information Administration
EPA	U.S. Environmental Protection Agency
EPRI	Electric Power Research Institute
FPL	Federal Poverty Level
GSP	Gross State Product
GWh	Gigawatt-hour
kWh	Kilowatt-hour
LBL	Lawrence Berkeley National Laboratory
LBNL	Lawrence Berkeley National Laboratory
LIHEAP	Low-Income Home Energy Assistance Program
MAPP	Mid-Continent Area Power Pool
MDOC	Minnesota Department of Commerce
MM	*mille-mille* (Million)
MSDC	Minnesota State Demographic Center
MW	Megawatt
NCAT	National Center for Appropriate Technology
NCLC	National Consumer Law Center
NERC	North American Electric Reliability Council
NO_X	Nitrogen Oxides

O3	Ozone
ORNL	Oak Ridge National Laboratory
PM10	Particulate Matter, 10 microns or less in diameter
PPI	Producer Price Index
RECS	Residential Energy Consumption Survey
SIC	Standard Industrial Classification
SO$_2$	Sulfur Dioxide
SOX	Sulfur Oxides
WAP	Weatherization Assistance Program

1. Introduction

Background

As in other states, energy conservation has been a policy goal in Minnesota since passage of the energy crisis–inspired legislation in the 1970s. The Minnesota Department of Commerce is responsible for advancing conservation through various programs and activities based on the finding that continued growth in energy demand is associated with adverse social and economic impacts, that minimizing the need for additional electricity generating plants is in the public interest, and that the state has a vital interest in providing for increased energy efficiency. The state's Conservation Improvement Program, enacted by the legislature in 1982, is Minnesota's leading conservation mandate. It requires state electric and gas utilities to spend a percentage of their annual income on conservation programs. During the period of 1996 to 1999, electric utilities spent $187.5 million, and gas utilities spent $47 million, for a savings of 1.3 billion kilowatt-hours of electricity and 4.3 billion cubic feet of natural gas. According to the American Council for an Energy-Efficient Economy (ACEEE), utility spending as a percentage of revenues was 1.16 percent in 1998, up from 1.13 percent in 1993 (Nadel, 2000).

In 1992, the federal Energy Policy Act expanded the authorization for nonutility companies to build and operate power plants that were established previously according to the Public Utility Regulatory Policies Act of 1978. In addition, the Federal Energy Regulatory Commission (FERC) Orders 888 and 889 in 1996 allowed competitive suppliers access to the bulk power transmission system. Thus, the industry continues to evolve toward a system of open competition according to various federal and state mandates. While the uncertainty associated with this transition has removed incentives for investment in energy efficiency as energy suppliers position themselves more competitively, the potential benefits of energy efficiency programs have not disappeared, even in a restructured market.

Research Approach

Independent from the studies performed by the Minnesota Department of Commerce, we assess the public benefits that accrue from improvements in energy efficiency and evaluate past and potential future benefits to the economy of Minnesota, its environment, and its citizens. We use panel data provided by the Department of Energy, Energy Information Administration, and present a model of benefits derived over the period 1977–1997. We also suggest potential future benefits through 2015 assuming continued encouragement of energy efficiency activities. While several benefits of energy efficiency have already been mentioned, this report addresses only three of these benefits:

- Effects on the gross state product (GSP) of energy efficiency improvements in the commercial and industrial sectors.

- Effects on air emissions of the improved utilization of energy in the commercial and industrial sectors.

- Effects on households, particularly low-income households, of improvements in residential energy efficiency.

Note that energy efficiency can take on two complementary notions: An energy efficient appliance in a home, for example, can use less energy to provide the same level of service, or it can use the same amount of energy to provide an increased level of service. In the first case, less energy is used, and the reduction can be measured directly. In the second case, the same amount of energy is used and to describe the increase in efficiency requires a measure of comfort or utility—characteristics that elude succinct and accurate definition and measurement. Energy efficiency, then, is a difficult metric to use directly.

In this report, we use measures of energy intensity as a proxy for energy efficiency. Defined broadly, energy intensity is the energy used per unit of output or unit served. An economywide indicator of energy intensity may be the energy per GSP. In the commercial sector, where the primary energy load is for lighting and space conditioning, an appropriate measure of energy intensity may be energy use per square foot, perhaps accounting for occupancy and employee hours.[1] In both these examples, changes in energy intensity reflect inverse changes in energy efficiency: When energy intensity decreases, energy efficiency increases. However, a change in energy intensity does not necessarily reflect a change in energy efficiency. In the industrial sector, for instance, a change in energy use per dollar of GSP may be due to changes in the mix of industries in the state or an increase in the price of energy rather than the investment in new equipment or energy efficient technologies. Energy efficiency, in this context, is defined as only those changes in energy intensity in the industrial and

---

[1]Primary electricity is a measurement of electricity that includes the approximate amount of energy used to generate electricity.

commercial sectors that are not due to economic or sectoral factors, such as energy price, capital investment, and climate.

The approach used in this study follows that of a previous RAND study for the California Energy Commission that examined the public benefit of energy efficiency to the state of California (Bernstein et al., 2000). Similarly, our analysis here adopts a macroeconomic view of the Minnesota economy with commercial and industrial energy intensity as key independent variables, and GSP as the dependent variable. We attempt to control for several potentially confounding factors, such as price, industrial mix, new capital, and climate. The empirical specification and results for Minnesota are detailed elsewhere (Bernstein et al., 2000) and are summarized in the appendix of this report. However, additional research is necessary to evaluate the validity of the underlying assumptions and the robustness of the economic analysis to modeling error. A second aspect of our analysis quantifies the effect of reduced energy intensity in the commercial and industrial sectors on air quality in Minnesota.

In addition to our analysis of GSP improvements associated with efficiency (i.e., energy intensity separate from the confounding factors mentioned above) in the commercial and industrial sectors, we examine energy efficiency benefits in the residential sector. Unlike the commercial and industrial sectors, the value of energy efficiency to the residential sector is not directly quantifiable. Therefore, we examine a number of benefits to Minnesota households due to energy efficiency, including financial savings, increased comfort, and increased energy services. We focus our analysis of the residential sector on low-income households because of their disproportionate energy burden relative to income level.

Together, the analyses described above provide useful evidence for estimating the value of energy efficiency to Minnesota.[2]

In summary, there are four key issues and assumptions in this report:

- This analysis shows that declines in energy intensity are associated with increases in GSP when sectoral composition, energy prices, and other factors remain constant.

- When these other factors are held constant, changes in energy intensity can be an approximation of changes in energy efficiency. Thus, the conclusion is

---

[2]While the transportation sector also accounts for a large and increasing portion of energy consumption in Minnesota, analysis of transportation sector energy use is beyond the scope of this study.

that improvements in energy efficiency are associated with improvements in gross state product.

- Government investments in energy efficiency programs may lead to improvements in GSP. At this point, we do not know how government programs affect the overall energy efficiency as used in the GSP analysis.

- Estimates of the cost per kilowatt-hour (kWh) saved by efficiency programs are compared with changes in GSP that appear to be the result of improvements in energy efficiency. These comparisons are informative, but we do not assume that the costs of energy efficiency programs translate dollar for dollar into costs saved for energy expenditures.

2. Trends in Minnesota Energy Intensity, Demand, and Environmental Factors

Energy Intensity and Energy Consumption Drivers

The following is a brief description of the past trends in energy intensity, as well as energy consumption drivers, in Minnesota, comparable states, and for the United States in general. These trends illustrate the energy setting in Minnesota and in the national context within which we have conducted our analysis and from which we can interpret our results. For comparison to Minnesota, the states of Illinois, New York, and California were selected.

Industrial Sector

The industrial sector is that subdivision of the economy that comprises manufacturing, agriculture, mining, construction, fishing, and forestry. Its components can be identified by their Department of Commerce Standard Industrial Classification (SIC) codes corresponding to these economic activities. In addition, the DOE (U.S. Department of Energy) has used a number of indicators of energy intensity to characterize changes in the energy consumption pattern in the industrial sector. These include energy use per gross product originating, per value added, per value of production, and per industrial production (DOE/EIA, 1995a). In our analysis, we use energy consumption per gross state product originating from the industrial sector. In this section, the energy intensities reported have not been controlled for the factors named above and thus may include combined effects of price, capital, labor, and other factors besides energy efficiency.

Figure 2.1 is a plot of energy intensity in the industrial sector in Minnesota, Illinois, New York, California, and the United States from 1977 to 1997. In Figure 2.1, we see that industrial energy intensity remained generally stable over the entire period, but declined between 1979 and 1987. Industrial energy intensity in Minnesota remained below the national average, but exceeded both California and New York during this period, and surpassed Illinois in the 1990s.

Differences in energy intensity can be explained, in part, by the mixture of industries in the industrial sector. Certain industrial activities require a

6

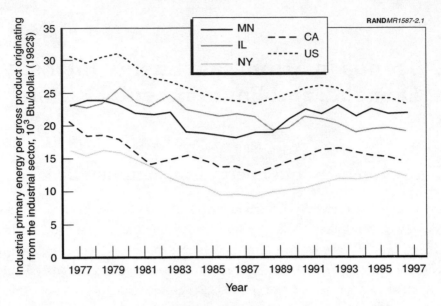

SOURCES: DOE/EIA, 1999a, 1999b; BEA, 1999.

Figure 2.1—Industrial Energy Consumption Per Gross State Product

significantly greater input of energy per dollar of output than others. Energy intensive industries include mining (SIC 30000); stone, clay, and glass (SIC 51320); primary metals (SIC 51330); paper products (SIC 52260); chemicals (SIC 52280); and petroleum products (SIC 52290). Figure 2.2 is a plot of the fraction of the gross industrial product produced from energy intensive industries in the four states of interest and the United States as a whole from 1977 to 1997. One can see from the plot that the share of Minnesota's industrial product originating from energy intensive industries has declined since 1977 and has generally exceeded that of New York and California during the study period. However, it remained below that of Illinois and of the national average. Shifts in the composition in the industrial sector are an important control factor in our analysis.

Recall that energy intensity is the ratio of a sector's energy consumption to its dollars of production; therefore, this ratio will, from year to year, increase if energy consumption increases at a faster rate than production. Likewise, if production increases at a faster rate than consumption, the energy intensity measure will decrease. From Figures 2.1 and 2.2, a decline in industrial energy intensity occurred in the 1980s that coincided with a shift away from energy intensive industry during this period. Figure 2.3 shows in more detail the overall consumption and production of the Minnesota industrial sector from 1977–1997. While the shift away from energy intensive industry may account for an increase

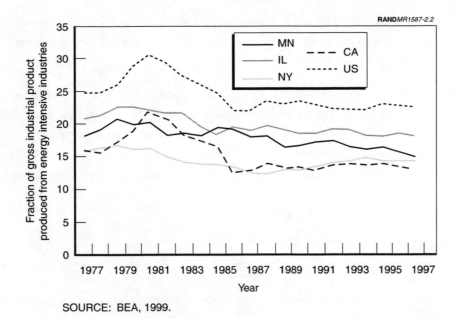

SOURCE: BEA, 1999.

**Figure 2.2—Fraction of Gross Industrial Product Produced from
Energy Intensive Industries**

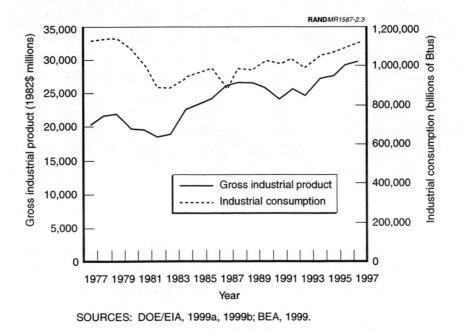

SOURCES: DOE/EIA, 1999a, 1999b; BEA, 1999.

**Figure 2.3—Total Industrial Consumption and Gross Industrial
Product, Minnesota**

in production relative to consumption in the 1980s, decreased energy intensity in the late 1970s also occurred and may be the result of more efficient industrial production during that time.

Historic declines in energy intensity have corresponded with high energy prices and implementation of demand-side-management (DSM) programs. Since the late 1980s, however, Minnesota has seen industrial energy intensity rise, corresponding to a reduction in the cost of energy, the early stages of reductions of DSM programs, and economic growth. Of these factors, high energy prices are not expected to persist, and without other incentives to reduce consumption, industrial energy intensity may continue to rise.

Commercial Sector

The commercial sector is considered to be the economic sector that is "neither residential, manufacturing/industrial, nor agricultural" (DOE/EIA, 1998b). As in the case of the industrial sector, there are a number of indicators of energy intensity that may be used to characterize the commercial sector's utilization of energy. Figure 2.4 is a plot of the energy consumption per gross state product in the commercial sector in Minnesota, Illinois, New York, California, and the United States. As with other states, commercial energy intensity in Minnesota has generally declined since the late 1970s. During the study period, Minnesota's commercial energy intensity remained below that of Illinois and the national average, but exceeded that of New York and California.

The commercial sector uses most of its energy for space conditioning and lighting. According to the DOE/EIA (1998b), "commercial buildings include, but are not limited to, the following: stores, offices, schools, churches, gymnasiums, libraries, museums, hospitals, clinics, warehouses, and jails." The energy used for space conditioning and lighting is a function, in part, of the amount of floor space in the commercial sector. Therefore, an alternative measure of energy intensity in the commercial sector is energy use per square foot. Figure 2.5 illustrates the primary energy consumption per square foot in the four states of interest from 1977 to 1997. Inspection of Figure 2.5 reveals that commercial energy consumption per square foot in Minnesota has fluctuated but has generally not declined since the 1970s.

While a state law was enacted in 1975 to require energy efficient building design and construction standards, individual counties outside the seven-county Minneapolis/St. Paul area and incorporated cities with a population of 2,500 or more were given the option to enforce the statewide building code in 1979. Many elected to have no enforcement within their area. Currently, these counties

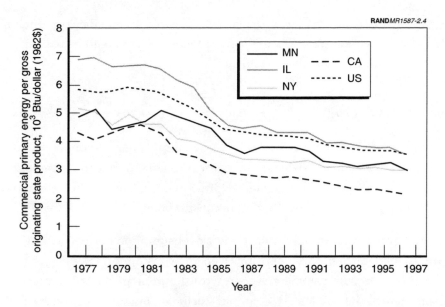

SOURCES: DOE/EIA, 1999a, 1999b; BEA, 1999.

Figure 2.4—Commercial Energy Consumption Per Gross State Product

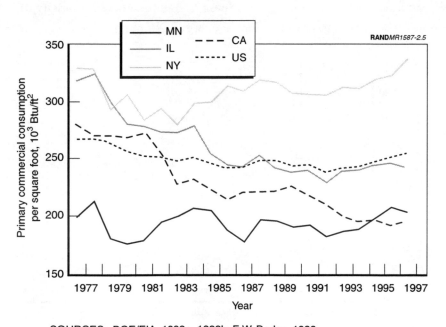

SOURCES: DOE/EIA, 1999a, 1999b; F. W. Dodge, 1999.

**Figure 2.5—Primary Commercial Energy Consumption Per Square Foot
of Nonresidential Floor Space**

and incorporated cities must adopt and enforce the state code, and enforcement
occurs for about 80 percent of the population. While increased compliance with

the state energy code may be expected to decrease commercial energy intensity, potentially lower energy prices in the future may contribute to increased commercial energy intensity as well.

Residential Sector

Although we do not analyze the residential sector in a macroeconomic analysis of the benefits of energy efficiency, a review of general trends in household energy consumption in Minnesota is helpful in understanding the residential energy setting and the factors that drive consumption.

Figure 2.6 shows the annual primary energy consumption per household, while Figure 2.7 illustrates the annual primary energy consumption per capita from 1977 to 1997. As with commercial energy consumption per square foot, energy consumption in the residential sector has fluctuated but generally has not declined since the 1970s. Both indicate a general decline in energy intensity over the study period, likely due in part to compliance with energy codes, especially for new construction. Through examinations of the expenditures on energy in the residential sector, we will connect these declines in energy intensity to benefits for several classes of residential energy customers.

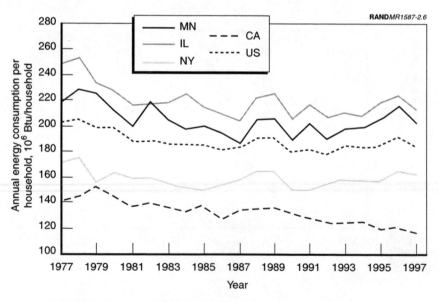

SOURCES: Census, 1999; DOE/EIA, 1999a, 1999b.

Figure 2.6—Annual Per-Household Energy Consumption for the United States and Selected States

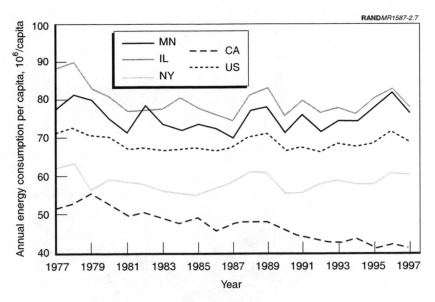

SOURCES: Census, 1999; DOE/EIA, 1999a, 1999b.

**Figure 2.7—Annual Residential Per-Capita Energy Consumption for
the United States and Selected States**

Demographic projections predict that Minnesota's population will increase by
more than 7 percent from 2000 to 2015, as shown in Figure 2.8, with greatest
growth in the nine suburban counties in the Minneapolis/St. Paul metropolitan
area (i.e., Anoka, Benton, Carver, Dakota, McLeod, Scott, Sherburne,
Washington, and Wright). Another area of anticipated growth includes the more
rural counties of Cass, Crow Wing, and Hubbard. Minnesotans live in a severe
climate zone with hot summers and cold winters. Cooling and heating loads are
greater in these areas; thus, businesses and residences located in these areas will
require higher energy intensities. Minnesota's rural households face especially
large energy burdens because of limited natural gas service and reliance on less
efficient electric heating and because of such electricity services as pumping
water and outdoor lighting, which are provided by municipalities in urban areas.

Energy intensity in the residential sector may be expected to decrease as new
buildings are built to comply with the state's energy code. Yet, lower energy
prices in the long term, use of new electronic household and office appliances,
and increased space-conditioning load could lead to increased energy intensity in
all sectors.

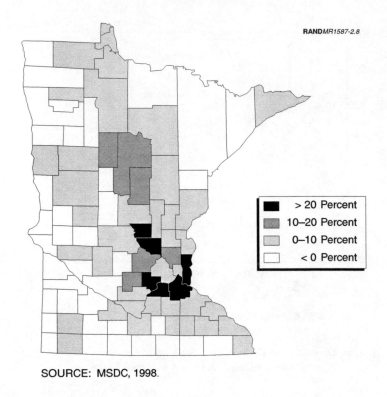

SOURCE: MSDC, 1998.

Figure 2.8—Forecasted Minnesota Population Growth by County, 2000–2015

Energy Demand and Reliability

Minnesota is within the Mid-Continent Area Power Pool (MAPP) region of the North American Electricity Reliability Council (NERC) system. This region includes North Dakota, Nebraska, Iowa, parts of Montana, South Dakota, Wisconsin, and the Canadian provinces of Saskatchewan and Manitoba. Minnesota is a net importer of electricity and, as such, is subject to regional reliability and demand conditions.

According to the NERC (2000), planned generation resources in the MAPP region are inadequate to supply the forecasted annual summer peak demand growth in the next ten years. Considering the uncertainty of forecasting, the MAPP region may have a deficit of capacity of 5,300 megawatts (MW) by the summer of 2009, while utilities have committed to providing only an additional 1,183 MW of capacity over this period (NERC, 2000). Although the MAPP transmission system is expected to operate near its secure limit, it is judged to be adequate to meet the needs of member systems and will continue to meet reliability criteria over the next ten years. However, potential restrictions may limit energy transfers from the Minneapolis-St. Paul area to Iowa and Wisconsin.

Reliability in the MAPP, and throughout North America, will depend in large part upon the smooth transition from bundled monopoly services to competition in wholesale and retail markets, according to federal and state restructuring laws. Obtaining the benefits of a competitive marketplace requires facing the challenges associated with interconnection, market power, and stranded cost recovery, while maintaining the reliability of the power system.

Environmental Factors

In the same way that the growth in Minnesota has increased energy demand in the state, it has also increased environmental pressure. Air quality, in particular, has decreased, especially near population centers. Further population growth in these areas and increased energy use will exacerbate air quality problems. As in other states, the primary contributor to decreased air quality throughout Minnesota is motor vehicles, but emissions from electricity production and industry also contribute to air pollution. In-state electricity production depends in large part on petroleum and coal-fired thermal generators; in fact, the proportion of electricity produced by coal-fired generation has remained relatively stable since 1988 (DOE/EIA, 2001). Most utilities in the MAPP region propose to install natural gas-fired combustion turbines to meet future capacity obligations (NERC, 1999).

Based on data from the Environmental Protection Agency, Figure 2.9 illustrates current areas of nonattainment status for criteria pollutants regulated under the Clean Air Act (EPA, 2001). Parts of Ramsey County are in nonattainment for particulate matter less than 10 microns in diameter (PM10), and parts of Olmsted County are in nonattainment for sulfur dioxide (SO2). It is important to note that the air quality is time dependent and that periods of poor air quality are the result of both natural and anthropogenic causes. Continued growth is expected in counties where air quality is already a concern.

Conclusions

Energy use in Minnesota has increased in the past and will continue to increase in the future. Energy planners in the state must continue to consider options for meeting this growing demand, beyond that which has been provided by the state's existing generation system and imports. In the following sections, we show that the declines in energy intensity in the industrial and commercial sectors have had cost-effective positive benefits for the state economy, its environmental quality, and its citizens. While the interplay of government regulations, efficiency programs, prices, climate, and economic factors that

14

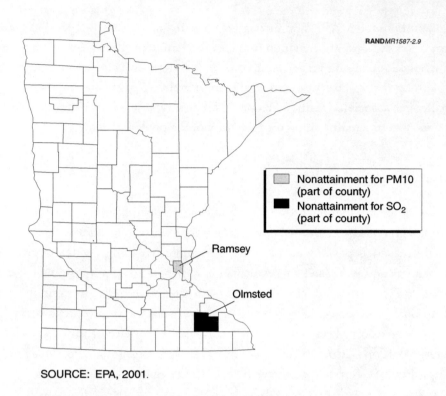

RAND*MR1587-2.9*

Ramsey

Olmsted

Nonattainment for PM10
(part of county)

Nonattainment for SO$_2$
(part of county)

SOURCE: EPA, 2001.

Figure 2.9—Minnesota Nonattainment Areas for PM10 and SO$_2$ by County in 2001

contributed to historic declines in energy intensity may not be present in the future, we argue that the potential benefits associated with decreased energy intensity may continue, especially with the encouragement of energy efficiency in the state.

3. Energy Efficiency in the Industrial and Commercial Sectors, Economic Growth, and Environmental Benefits

This section presents our analysis of the benefits of energy efficiency in the industrial and commercial sectors for the economic output of the state, or GSP, from 1977 to 1997. We compare this benefit with the investments and savings of selected utility energy-efficiency programs over this period. We also speculate about potential future benefits of energy efficiency in the commercial and industrial sectors. Finally, we examine some of the environmental benefits of energy efficiency.

Energy Efficiency and the Minnesota Economy: 1977–1997

Our econometric analysis estimates the average effect of energy intensity and other factors on GSP in the 48 contiguous states. To determine the estimated effects for Minnesota, we use the national averages on data from 1979 to 1997 as a baseline for determining the effects of changes in energy intensity—while controlling for energy price, sectoral composition, and other factors—on Minnesota's per-capita economic growth.

The analysis shows that changes in energy intensity are associated with the growth of GSP. As illustrated in appendix Table A.5, from 1979 to 1997 GSP per capita in Minnesota grew from $19,294 to $32,229. According to the analysis, if energy intensity had remained constant at the 1979 level over this period, then GSP per capita would have been 2.8 percent less than its actual 1997 value. Figure 3.1 shows the actual evolution of GSP per capita and the predicted evolution in the case of constant energy intensity.

As shown in Table 3.1, this economic growth is equivalent to $903 per capita in 1997. When we examine the impact of energy intensity, controlling for various exogenous factors across states with industrial characteristics similar to Minnesota, we find that the impact on GSP per capita is $824 per capita.

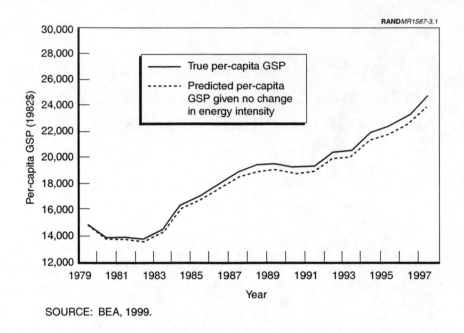

RAND*MR1587-3.1*

SOURCE: BEA, 1999.

Figure 3.1—Actual GSP Per Capita and GSP Per Capita in the Case of Constant Energy Intensity

Table 3.1

The Estimated Effects of Energy Intensity Improvements on the Minnesota Economy

Effect of Energy Intensity on the Minnesota Economy	Increase in 1997 GSP Per Capita	Increase in Total GSP in 1997 (billions)	Increase in Total GSP, 1979–1997 (billions)
National average	$903	$4.2	$37.5
States similar to Minnesota	$824	$3.9	$33.9

The Value of Energy Efficiency Programs to Minnesota

Since the 1980s, there have been state- and utility-sponsored energy efficiency programs in Minnesota. Often, these programs target specific end users and end uses, such as lighting, home insulation, and facility retrofitting. The purpose of the programs is to promote cost-effective energy efficiency improvements in the state's industries, stores, offices, farms, and homes. In order to draw solid conclusions about the impact of energy efficiency programs on GSP, we need to include in our model data related to the expenditures for these programs as an explanatory variable. Absent these data, we take an indirect approach. In this subsection we compare increases in GSP to estimates of energy and monetary savings reported for state-sponsored energy efficiency programs in Minnesota, although we recognize that the extent to which the programs have actually contributed to declines in energy intensity is unknown.

The previous subsection showed that since 1977, reductions in energy intensity have been associated with economic gains of $903 per capita, or approximately $4.2 billion in 1997. In fact, the cumulative gains over the entire period amount to approximately $37.5 billion. Likewise, we can estimate the amount of energy that would have been consumed had energy intensity remained constant over the time period, and we can describe this savings in terms of dollars per unit of energy saved ($/GWh). This number serves as a rough benchmark for comparison to DSM program costs. Note that these are savings only due to energy intensity improvements in the commercial and industrial sectors, and it is assumed that the energy saved is the result of changes in energy intensity independent of the control factors. From modeled benefits to GSP over the study period, in terms of $/GWh, and utility investment and savings rates, also in terms of $/GWh, we can make an informative comparison of benefits to costs. Note, however, that we cannot make conclusions about the effectiveness of utility conservation programs, since we have not shown a specific link between investment in energy efficiency programs and effects on energy intensity.

Unfortunately, the data that describe the expenditures and energy savings of DSM programs is limited. Wide-scale reporting by the utilities generally did not occur prior to 1990, and data describing investment and savings for commercial and industrial programs in Minnesota span only the years from 1996 to 1998. Therefore, we used data describing investment and savings for commercial and industrial programs for the period 1996–1999, as reported by the state's utilities and compiled by the Minnesota Department of Commerce (MDOC, 2001). RAND has not independently verified these estimates.

Furthermore, utility estimates of costs and energy savings have been reported in terms of annual dollar costs and first-year electricity savings. We must therefore assume an average program life since an investment must correspond to energy savings over the life of a program. Based on related RAND research in other states (California, Washington, and Massachusetts), we believe that it is not unreasonable to assume a program life of ten years.

According to utility reports, we find that Minnesota utilities invested $73.9 million in commercial and industrial energy efficiency programs between 1996 and 1999, achieving approximately 29,868 GWh of energy savings over the life of these programs. This is an average rate of approximately $2,655/GWh (0.27 cents/kWh). Our model results for Minnesota show increases to GSP of $9.7

billion corresponding to 275,646 GWh of savings ($35,368/GWh, or 3.5 cents/kWh). If utility estimates of investment and savings in conservation programs are, in fact, indicative of investment and savings in energy efficiency activities in Minnesota and if energy intensity in the commercial and industrial sector has indeed been affected by the programs, then such a comparison favors these programs. However, to determine the relationship between energy efficiency programs and changes in energy intensity, and to identify an actual return on investment, would require additional analysis. It is important to note that the notion of a return on investment in this context applies to the state economy as a whole and not to those who participated in energy efficiency programs in particular.

Although we do not know the true benefits of conservation programs with certainty, nor do we know the effect of such programs on energy intensity, we may ask how accurately the utilities must report investment and savings in order for the programs to be cost-effective compared with our benchmark ($35,368/GWh, or 3.5 cents/kWh). Our analysis suggests that had these programs saved only 8 percent of the savings that were reported, the unit cost of energy ($/GWh) of such programs would have been roughly equivalent to our predicted savings to the state. Thus, the programs were cost-effective, even if their energy savings were overestimated by an order of magnitude.

We must note that the difference between program cost and the value of savings in Minnesota is quite high. In particular, we found the reported costs of conservation programs in Minnesota to be exceptionally low in comparison with other states we have studied. This could be a result of many factors, including the local climate and types of programs typically employed in Minnesota. In addition, it is unclear how much of the true cost of the programs was borne by the utilities. It is entirely plausible that the utilities are reporting only their own portion of each program's cost along with all energy savings attributable to the programs. To clarify these issues would require more detailed data and further analysis.

Future Benefits of Energy Efficiency to Minnesota

In the previous subsection we showed that improvements in energy intensity, perhaps influenced by energy efficiency programs, are associated with economic benefits to the state. In what follows, we project our results into the future (2015) and determine the future value of energy efficiency while making some assumptions regarding future changes in energy intensity.

In the past, improvements in energy efficiency often coincided with
improvements in industry practice and investment in new equipment and
processes. Yet with the rapid advance of technology and changes in energy
services, it is possible that Minnesota's gains in energy intensity may reverse.
Therefore, we consider a set of future scenarios based on possible changes in
energy intensity in the commercial and industrial sectors. These projections
cannot be tied directly to the funds that may be spent on energy efficiency in the
future, but they do allow us to speculate regarding the continued benefits of
energy efficiency to the Minnesota economy.

Inspection of Figures 2.1 and Figure 2.4 suggests three general trends in energy
intensity in Minnesota. From 1977 to 1997, energy intensity in both the industrial
and commercial sectors generally declined. However, two phases of energy
intensity changes occurred during this greater period: From 1977 to 1987, energy
intensity in Minnesota decreased in both commercial and industrial sectors, but
from 1987 to 1997, the average industrial energy intensity increased. These
changes are due in part to shifts in industrial mix, but gains in energy efficiency
have also contributed. Figure 3.2 presents three possible future scenarios as
extrapolations of trends in energy intensity changes for the industrial and
commercial sectors.

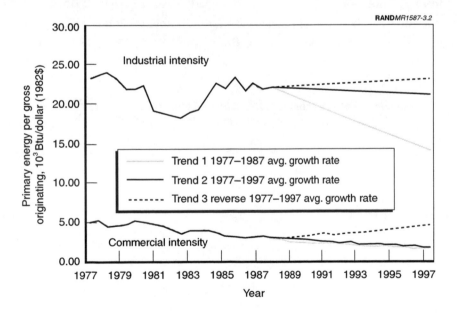

**Figure 3.2—Trends of Primary Energy Intensity in Minnesota in
the Industrial and Commercial Sectors**

In one scenario, energy intensity decreases as it did from 1977 to 1987. In the second scenario, energy intensity declines only moderately according to the 1977–1997 average change. In the third scenario, energy intensity increases as if the overall 1977–1997 trend had reversed itself. Using the national average coefficients calculated previously, we estimate expected economic growth for each of the three scenarios. In addition, we calculate low and high estimates for the effect of energy intensity on the state economy based on the standard error of our estimate. Recall that these coefficients were derived from our analysis and controlled for price, sectoral composition, and other factors. We compare these nine results against a baseline that assumes no change in energy intensity from 1997. Table 3.2 presents the nine estimates of the changes in GSP per capita due to the combined effects of changes in commercial and industrial energy intensity under these three scenarios.

Our analysis shows that if energy intensity in the commercial and the industrial sectors reverses its 1977–1997 trend, the cumulative net loss in GSP per capita by 2015 could be about $456 per capita as compared with the baseline. On the other hand, the analysis shows that reductions of energy intensity can continue to have large-scale economic benefits to the state: if energy intensity in Minnesota continues to decline at its average rate from 1977–1997, we could expect an additional increase in GSP per capita between $75 and $846 by 2015, depending on the estimated benefits of decreased energy intensity. Better still, if energy intensity in Minnesota declines according to the 1977–1987 trend, we could

Table 3.2

Estimates of Future Economic Benefits of Reductions in Energy Intensity to Minnesota in Terms of Per-Capita GSP

		2015 Changes in GSP Per Capita from 1997		
		1977–1987 Trend	1977–1997 Trend	Reverse 1977–1997 Trend
Estimate of the Effect of Energy Intensity on the Minnesota Economy	1997 Benefits	Large Decrease in Energy Intensity	Moderate Decrease in Energy Intensity	Increase in Energy Intensity
National Average— High Impact	$1,115	$1,758	$846	–$834
National Average— Middle Impact	$903	$1,026	$459	–$456
National Average— Low Impact	$690	$303	$75	–$75

expect an additional increase in GSP per capita between $303 and $1,758 per capita, depending on the estimated benefits of decreased energy intensity. Note that these measures of energy intensity include the controls we used in our analysis.

If one believes that energy intensity could increase rather than decrease, as it did in 1977–1997, and that energy efficiency programs can achieve improvements similar to those made from 1977-1997, the potential benefit could be $915 per capita (the difference of the average values in column four and column five of Table 3.2.) In a state of 4.9 million residents (Census, 1999), the potential gain in GSP in 2015 could range from $738 million (using the low values under these same assumptions) to $8.3 billion (using the high values under these assumptions).

Environmental Benefits of Reduced Energy Intensity

Environmental policy and regulatory requirements associated with electricity generation are many and complex. Potential environmental impacts such as air emissions, hazardous waste, poor water quality, and land-use disputes are all areas of concern.

In this analysis, we focus on the effects of energy consumption on air quality. In particular, energy consumption directly leads to air emissions, including various air pollutants regulated under the Clean Air Act (e.g., particulate matter, SO_2, NO_X, CO) and CO_2. We calculate emissions reductions due to reduced energy intensity in the industrial and commercial sectors from the total electricity used in each sector, and we compare this reduced usage with the electricity consumption that would have occurred if energy intensity had not changed since 1977. We also consider the fact that Minnesota receives its power from a variety of sources in the MAPP region; thus, emissions rates and the state's total emissions from electricity consumption are calculated from the aggregate emissions in that region. Finally, we look at the aggregate emissions from fossil-fueled generators in that region because, in general, those would be the emitters that would most likely be reduced, or increased, in any one year.

If we consider an aggregate emissions level from fossil-fueled power production in the MAPP, reduced energy intensity in the commercial and industrial sectors displaced approximately 28,000 tons of SO_2 and 19,000 tons of NO_X. In addition, CO_2 emissions were reduced from approximately 50 million tons to approximately 43 million tons in 1997 as a result of reduced energy intensity in commercial and industrial sectors in Minnesota (see Figure 3.3).

22

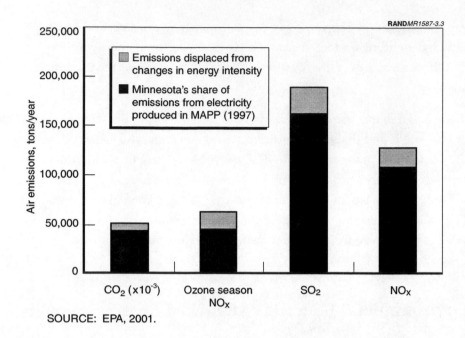

SOURCE: EPA, 2001.

**Figure 3.3—Emission Reductions from Electricity Produced in the MAPP
Due to Changes in Energy Efficiency in Minnesota**

Air quality has decreased in Minnesota, particularly near growing population centers. As shown in Figure 2.9, parts of Ramsey County are in nonattainment of PM10 standards, and parts of Olmsted County are in nonattainment of SO_2 standards (EPA, 2001). Increased population growth will exacerbate problems in air quality due to energy use. While the primary contributors to decreased air quality throughout Minnesota are motor vehicles, emissions from electricity production and industry also contribute. Our analysis shows that reductions in energy intensity have not only produced economic benefits but have also slowed the increase in air emissions throughout the state.

4. Benefits of Energy Efficiency in the Residential Sector

While changes in GSP due to changes in energy intensity may indicate benefits from commercial and industrial energy efficiency, no convenient macroeconomic indicator is available that can quantify the benefits to the state economy from energy efficiency in the residential sector. We can, however, look at the benefits to households. The following discussion describes some of the benefits to Minnesota households from reductions in household energy intensity. These benefits include financial savings, increased comfort, and an increased number of energy services. Our comparison of household energy consumption and expenditures in Minnesota with those of other states and across income levels suggests that reductions in household energy intensity have benefited the state's citizens, particularly those of low-income households in less temperate parts of the state.

Residential Energy Consumption Characteristics

As in the industrial and commercial sectors, changes in residential energy consumption are due to a number of factors, including climate, size of household, age of the home and its appliances, the presence and enforcement of a residential energy code, and the price of energy. Previously, we presented two indicators of energy efficiency for the aggregate residential sectors in Minnesota, Illinois, New York, California, and the United States in general—i.e., residential energy consumption per household (Figure 2.6) and residential energy consumption per capita (Figure 2.7).

Table 4.1 lists the percentage changes in per-capita primary energy consumption[1] in Minnesota, Illinois, New York, and California according to Ortiz and Bernstein (1999). Also included is the year in which the state adopted a residential energy-efficiency building code. Accordingly, primary residential energy consumption per capita in Minnesota has fallen by approximately 3.3 percent since the 1970s. Similarly, in Illinois and New York, primary energy consumption per capita has decreased by approximately 5.5 and 3.5 percent, respectively, and California has

---

[1]Primary energy consumption describes consumption of energy with respect to its source, as opposed to consumption at its end use. Primary energy, thus, exceeds end use energy in that it also accounts for system and transmission losses.

Table 4.1

**Changes in Residential Primary Energy Consumption Per Capita,
Excluding Transportation**

State	Year of Residential Energy-Code Implementation	Percentage Change in Per-Capita Energy Consumption from 1970–1978 Average to 1988–1995 Average
IL	no code	–5.5
MN	1976	–3.3
NY	1979	–3.5
CA	1978	–19.2

SOURCE: Ortiz and Bernstein, 1999.

seen declines in excess of 19 percent. Thirty-five states in the United States have residential energy codes, and the average change in annual per-capita energy consumption for the 48 contiguous states over the same period has been a 1.7 percent increase.

In Minnesota, the changes in per-capita energy consumption have reduced real per-capita energy expenditures in the state. The history of real residential energy expenses appears in Figure 4.1. The 1992 residential energy expenses per capita in Minnesota were $477[2] (DOE/EIA, 1998a). The 1992 expenses represent a 33 percent decline in real energy expenses from the high of $718 in 1982. In a state of 4.7 million residents, the $241 annual per-capita savings per year from 1982 to 1992 translates into a gross savings to Minnesota residents of $1.1 billion. This savings includes a combination of both improvements in energy efficiency as well as energy prices, which have generally decreased in real terms over the study period.

Energy Efficiency and Low-income Households

Energy needs differ among households, with annual expenses for energy varying between approximately $1,000 and $2,000. Higher-income households tend to use more energy than lower-income households; however, the percentage of household income devoted to energy services is greater for low-income households. According to the 1997 Residential Energy Consumption Survey (RECS), the national average energy expenditures in 1997 for a household in the $5,000 to $9,999 income bracket were $985 ($1,000 in 1998$). However, for a

---

[2]For comparison in real terms, the energy savings to residential consumers have been adjusted according to the Consumer Price Index and are reported in 1998 dollars (1998$).

25

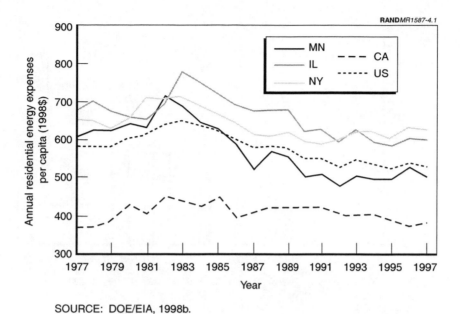

SOURCE: DOE/EIA, 1998b.

Figure 4.1—Real Energy Expenses Per Capita in the Residential Sector in Minnesota

household in the $75,000 and above income bracket, the expenditures were $1,864; see Figure 4.2. Thus, average energy expenditures in the highest income group are almost twice that of the lowest income group, but the income of the highest group is more than seven and a half times greater.

Furthermore, the realization of any savings in the residential sector is a function of the pattern of energy utilization in the household. When we compare expenditures by end use, we find that as much as two-thirds of energy-related expenditures are for the principal end uses of space conditioning, water heating, and refrigeration (see Figure 4.3). We consider these end uses to be essential energy services since they are shared across all income classes. The nationwide average expenditures per household for these services was $725 in 1997 for households with incomes less than $10,000 and $876 for households with incomes between $25,000 and $49,999—a 20 percent increase for a three-to-five-times greater household income. Savings, therefore, in essential energy services with respect to total household energy expenses will be more beneficial financially to the lower-income household than to other households, and the comfort and utility derived from essential energy services will be more sensitive to energy price and equipment efficiency in lower-income households than in higher-income households. As a result, energy savings may also have a greater effect on disposable income of lower-income households. For a more complete survey of low-income household expenditures on energy, refer to Bernstein et al.

26

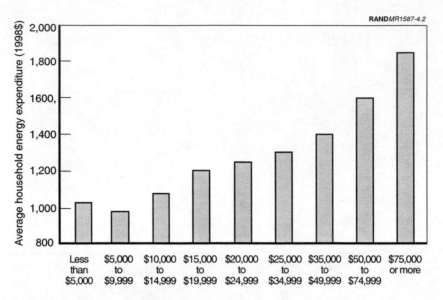

SOURCES: DOE/EIA, 1999a, 1999b.

**Figure 4.2—Nationwide Average Annual Energy Expenditures
Per Household by Income Level**

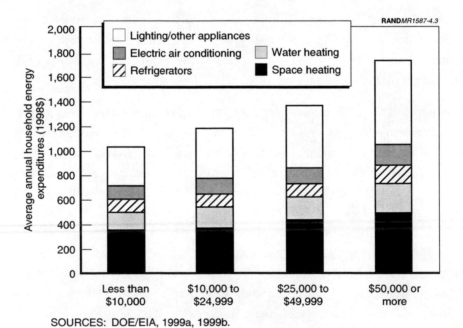

SOURCES: DOE/EIA, 1999a, 1999b.

**Figure 4.3—Nationwide Average Annual Energy Expenditures
by End Use and Household Income**

(2000). In general, we conclude that while residential energy efficiency improvements provide benefits to all households, lower-income households are especially sensitive to energy costs, and so the benefits are more significant for these households.

The disproportionate energy burden already borne by low-income households is exacerbated by their relatively inefficient use of energy; the housing occupied by low-income households tends to be older than the average and, therefore, designed and built in a less energy efficient manner and equipped with less energy efficient fixtures and appliances. A study of low-income households found that 64 percent of households with less than $5,000 annual income have ceiling insulation, compared with 91 percent of households with more than $50,000 annual income, and that 14 percent of the former group versus 5 percent of the latter group have a refrigerator that is more than 20 years old (Chandrasekar et al., 1994). Among residences heated primarily with natural gas, those built since 1980 use 43 percent less energy than those built between 1940 and 1979 (DOE/EIA, 1995a).

Overall, the poverty rate in Minnesota (7.8 percent, on average over the period 1998–2000) is below the comparable national average of 11.9 percent (Census, 1999). The greatest levels of poverty are found within a cluster of counties in the north-central part of the state, and include Beltrami (18.9 percent), Cass (15.3 percent), Clearwater (19.1 percent), Mahnomen (20.5 percent), and Wadena (16.2 percent). Figure 4.4 shows the percentage of people living in poverty in counties of Minnesota.

Minnesota, in general, is located in an extreme climate zone with hot, humid summers and cold winters. January minimum temperatures, normalized over a 30-year study period, range from approximately 0 degrees Fahrenheit (°F) in the southern part of the state, to –13 °F on the northern border; July maximum normalized temperatures are approximately 83 °F in the southern part of the state, and 78 °F on the northern border. In general, rural households in Minnesota have limited natural gas service and so must rely on more-expensive propane gas and less-efficient electric heating. Furthermore, they must use electricity for services such as water pumping and outdoor lighting that are provided by municipalities in urban areas. Thus, relative energy burdens on low-income, rural households in Minnesota remain large: The typical low-income household spends $1,102 per year on energy, compared with an average for median-income households of $1,289. Low-income households (below 150 percent of the federal poverty level—FPL) spend approximately 14.9 percent of their income on energy, whereas only 3.1 percent of income is spent on energy in median-income households (NCLC, 1995). Both summer cooling and winter

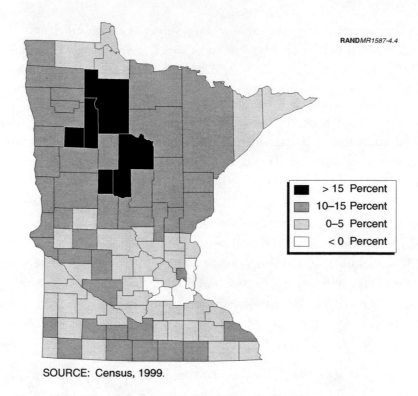

> 15 Percent
10–15 Percent
0–5 Percent
< 0 Percent

SOURCE: Census, 1999.

Figure 4.4—Percentage of Families in Minnesota Living in Poverty

heating loads are high in Minnesota, and they are greater outside the Minneapolis/St. Paul urban area. For example, the average electricity bill for low-income households in Minneapolis during the summer of 1992 was $265 (1998$), and $246 in the winter of 1992/1993. By comparison, the average electricity bill in Albert Lea, near the Iowa border, was $13 dollars higher in the summer and $35 dollars higher in the winter (Colton, 1994).

Based on estimates of energy expenditures by income level (DOE/EIA, 1999b) and estimates of savings associated with energy efficiency improvements such as weatherization (Berry, Brown, and Kinney, 1997), Figure 4.5 shows the energy expenditures in Minnesota households by income level and the potential reduction of energy expenditures with energy efficiency improvements; Figure 4.6 shows the energy burden (expenditure as a percentage of income) on Minnesota households by income level, and the potential reduction of this burden due to improvements in energy efficiency.

In recognition of these energy burdens, numerous federal, state, and utility-administered programs have sought to reduce energy costs, by direct financial assistance and through energy efficiency programs. The federal Weatherization Assistance Program (WAP) was established in 1974 under the Community

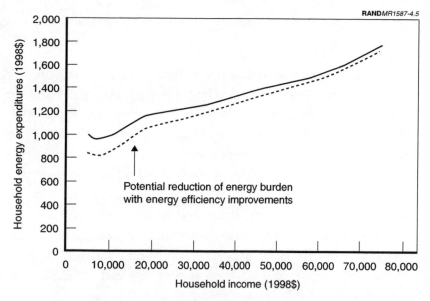

SOURCES: DOE/EIA, 1999b; Barry, Brown, and Kinney, 1997.

Figure 4.5—Minnesota Household Energy Expenditures as a Percentage of Income

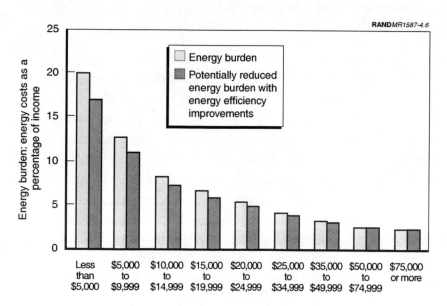

SOURCES: DOE/EIA, 1999b; Berry, Brown, and Kinney, 1997.

Figure 4.6—Minnesota Household Energy Expenditure as a Percentage of Income and Potential Reduction of Energy Burden with Energy Efficiency Improvements

Services Act to reduce the cost of heating and cooling by improving the energy efficiency of buildings.

A 1997 metaevaluation of numerous state weatherization programs under WAP showed that benefit-cost ratios increased on the order of 80 percent between 1989 and 1996 because of more complete audits and better and more effectively targeted improvements (Berry, Brown, and Kinney, 1997). Various perspectives of benefits were employed, from one-year savings on energy bills to 20-year returns on societal benefits. In 1996. the average benefit-cost ratio for first-year energy savings was 1.79. In the study, all of Minnesota was included in the "cold" climate belt, although we have noted earlier that there are differences in climate between the northern and southern areas of the state; Table 4.2 shows the average percentage reductions in home energy costs for households in the "cold" climate region after weatherization. Average benefit-to-cost ratios, depending on the perspective, were 1.3 to 2.9 in this region.

A detailed study of low-income weatherization programs nationwide found that, in general, the more that is invested in weatherizing a dwelling, the greater the savings (Berry and Brown, 1996). More important, savings were found to be linear with costs over the entire range of the data, with no evidence of diminishing returns.

Aside from weatherization, other low-income energy efficiency measures include installation of compact fluorescent light bulbs, which use approximately 70 percent less energy than incandescent bulbs; and refrigerator replacement, which can lower electricity bills by $500 to $1,000 over the unit's lifetime. The federal Low-Income Home Energy Assistance Program (LIHEAP), administered by the Department of Health and Human Services, was established in 1980 to reduce the burden of energy costs; to improve health, safety, and comfort; and to prevent termination of energy services. LIHEAP provides block grants to states and other administrative bodies, which in turn apply their own selection criteria within the federal guidelines. Nationally, funding for LIHEAP declined from approximately $2.1 billion in 1985 to $900 million in 1996; perhaps not coincidentally, the number of service terminations has doubled since 1988 as well

Table 4.2

First-Year Reduction in Home Energy Costs

	Electricity		Natural Gas	
Climate	Space Heating	Total	Space Heating	Total
"Cold"	42%	14%	25%	18%

SOURCE: Berry, Brown, and Kinney, 1997.

(Pye, 1996). In response to recent price shocks, LIHEAP funding has increased to approximately $1.3 billion in 2001 (NCAT, 2001a). In 1997, Minnesota was allotted $37.5 million and also received $13.7 million in emergency funds that year (DHHS, 1999). More recent energy price shocks have created new political support for LIHEAP funding—with 2001 allotments of $54.4 million and emergency funds of $34.8 million to Minnesota. Yet, LIHEAP served only 25 percent of the eligible population in the late 1990s in Minnesota (NCAT, 2001a, 2001b). While a full cost-effectiveness analysis of low-income energy efficiency programs in Minnesota is beyond the scope of this report, many of these types of programs nationwide have been shown to be cost-effective (Pye, 1996).

The more efficient the home the less the expenditure on energy. In this respect, low-income households benefit from having more disposable income, as do all households. But low-income households derive a broader set of benefits from a reduced energy burden. These benefits include increased comfort and health, appliance safety, reduced loss of service from termination, and increased value to property owners. Some of the cost savings from energy efficiency may be reinvested in increased usage; for example, if a residence is better insulated so as to increase the energy efficiency of air conditioning, the household may spend the same amount as previously on air conditioning but have more comfort. (Brown, Berry, and Kinney, 1994).

Benefits from greater energy efficiency for low-income households may go beyond the direct benefit to the households. These benefits may include reduced arrearages, increases in the quality of housing, and possibly an improved local economy (Howat and Oppenheim, 1999).

5. Conclusions

Our analysis shows that changes in energy intensity—controlled for such exogenous factors as price, industrial mix, and capital expenditures—are associated with important economic and environmental benefits for Minnesota and its citizens from 1979 to 1997. It is possible that these benefits can continue into the future. These benefits occurred in the presence of investment in energy efficiency programs by the government, the private sector, and state residents. Further research is necessary to describe the specific link between mandated government or voluntary private energy-efficiency programs and improvements in energy intensity in the state.

Past evaluations of energy-efficiency programs targeted at the commercial and industrial sectors, however, indicate that the programs can be directly responsible for energy savings. In fact, we have shown that claimed savings of commercial and industrial energy-efficiency programs have provided a positive return on utility investment, assuming that this return has been revealed in our controlled analysis of changes in energy intensity and that our limited data on utility investment and savings are indicative of the wider range of utility conservation programs. Future programs that have similar success rates as those of their predecessors would likely result in continued economic benefits to the state.

In addition, we have demonstrated benefits of energy efficiency for Minnesota households—particularly for low-income households in eastern Minnesota. Energy-efficiency programs that focus on residential consumers can directly increase both net income and quality of life for those consumers.

The future of energy consumption, prices, and intensity remains uncertain. The analysis here suggests that greater energy efficiency has had, and may continue to have, a positive effect on the Minnesota economy. Together, targeted energy-efficiency programs in commercial, industrial, and residential sectors have the potential to continue to provide benefits to the state, and they remain a cost-effective option for meeting the state's increasing energy demand. Specifically, how these programs affect aggregate energy intensity remains a subject of further research.

Appendix

This appendix summarizes the quantitative results of our analysis of economic impacts of changes in commercial and industrial energy intensity. This study employs a methodology used in a previous RAND study that examined the public benefit of energy efficiency to the state of California (Bernstein et al., 2000). We refer the reader to that study for more detailed discussion of the theory behind the methodology.

Empirical Specification

We consider the following regression specification:

$$EI_{it} = \beta_1 P_{it}^e + \beta_2 EM_{it} + \beta_3 K_{it} + \beta_4 C_{it} + \lambda_i + \nu_t + \varepsilon_{it} \qquad \text{(A.1)}$$

where i indexes states, t indexes time, and the variables are all in log form and defined as follows:

EI Energy intensity in the industrial sector taking the form E_{it}/Y_{it}, where E is energy consumption and Y represents industrial output (10^3 Btu/$).[1]

P^e Real energy prices in the industrial sector ($/$10^6$ Btu).

EM Proportion of industrial output accounted for by energy-intensive manufacturing. In the regression results below, non-mining manufacturing intensity (*Manufacturing*) and mining intensity (*Mining*) are allowed to have separate effects.[2]

K New capital expenditures (buildings and equipment) in the industrial sector ($$10^6$)

C An index of heating and cooling days.

λ A state fixed effect.

ν A time fixed effect.

---

[1] Except as otherwise noted, all economic variables are deflated using the Producer Price Index for Finished Goods and are expressed in 1982 dollars in this appendix.

[2] Energy-intensive manufacturing industries include mining (30000), stone, clay, and glass (51320), primary metals (51330), paper products (52260), chemicals (52280), and petroleum products (52290).

34

Our approach is to use energy intensity directly as a proxy for energy efficiency. To be concrete, consider the following model of GSP:

$$\Delta_t \ln \text{GSP}_{it} = \alpha_0 + \Delta_{t-1} \ln EI_i \alpha_1 + \Delta_{t-1} \ln P_i^e \alpha_2 + \Delta_{t-1} \ln EM_i \alpha_3$$
$$+ \Delta_{t-1} \ln K_i \alpha_4 + \Delta_{t-1} \ln C_i \alpha_5 + \Delta_t \ln X_i \alpha_6 + \lambda_i + \nu_t + \varepsilon_{it} \quad \text{(A.2)}$$

where Δ_t denotes first differences between periods t and $t-1$ (e.g., $\Delta_t \ln GSP_{it} = \ln GSP_{i,t} - \ln GSP_{i,t-1}$) and Δ_{t-1} denotes first differences between periods $t-1$ and $t-2$. The variables in the model are defined as follows:

GSP   Per-capita gross state product ($\$10^6$).

EI   A vector of energy-intensity variables taking the form E_{ijt}/Y_{ijt}, where E_j represents the energy consumption in sector j (industrial, commercial, and transportation) in Btus and Y_j represents the output of that sector (10^3 Btus/\$).

P^e A vector of real energy prices in the industrial, commercial, and transportation sectors ($\$/10^6$).

EM   Proportion of industrial output accounted for by energy-intensive manufacturing (*Manufacturing* and *Mining*).

K   A vector of new capital expenditures in the industrial sector (*new capital*, $\$10^6$) and stock of commercial building square footage (*Building*, ft^2).

C   An index of heating and cooling days.

X   A vector of additional covariates typically included in cross-state growth regressions—proportion of the population of working age (18–65), proportion of the population with a college-level education or more, service share of output, and government expenditures as a fraction of total output.

λ A state fixed effect.

ν A time fixed effect.

This specification follows a large literature on the determinants of economic growth.[3] It argues that per-capita state economic growth is correlated with both the stock and flow of capital and labor, their quality, and governmental policies. The inclusion of state fixed effects accounts for differences in initial economic

---

[3]Standard references include Solow (1957), Dennison (1962), Barro and Sala-i-Martin (1995), Griliches (1998), and Jorgenson, Gollop, and Fraumeni (1987). See Crain and Lee (1999) for a review of the empirical literature on the determinants of U.S. state economic growth.

conditions and governmental policies (separate from expenditures) that affect economic growth. Time fixed effects control for business cycle effects common to all states.

Results for the Nation

Table A.3 presents our baseline regression results for the effect of changes in the growth rate of industrial and commercial energy intensity (Table A.1) on state economic growth. The coefficients (Table A.2) on industrial and commercial energy intensity (–0.023 and –0.017) indicate that GSP growth rises as state economies become less energy intensive. These estimates tell us that a 10 percent increase in the rate of growth in industrial energy intensity, for example, leads to a 0.23 percent decline in the rate of state economic growth. The remaining covariates in the model generally have signs and magnitudes consistent with the literature on state economic growth. One exception is the coefficient estimate on *new capital*. Investment is generally thought to be the cornerstone of economic growth, and so it is somewhat puzzling that *new capital* is statistically insignificant. This is at odds with the literature on economic growth in general, although the measurement of industrial capital is generally difficult and the particular measure used here is different from those employed in other studies of state economic growth.[4] Also, as noted above, the effect of any measurement error in this variable, which tends to bias the coefficient toward zero, will be exacerbated using first differences and state fixed effects. Note that the addition of new commercial buildings, a variable that is easier to quantify than industrial capital, has the expected sign and is of a substantial magnitude.

Although, at first glance, these coefficients appear small, their cumulative effects on the level of state GSP over time can be quite large. This is because growth is an exponential process. Table A.4 illustrates the predicted effect of energy intensity on state economic growth using data on GSP and energy intensity averaged across the 48 states in our analysis. The first three columns list the mean values of *Ind. EI*, *Com. EI*, and per-capita GSP. The fourth column estimates what per-capita income would have been had there been no change in energy intensity between 1979 and 1997.[5] Actual per-capita GSP in 1997 was $22,363. Had there been no change in energy intensity, the model predicts per-capita GSP in 1997 would have been $21,746. Thus, we can conclude that the decline in industrial and commercial energy intensity between 1979 and 1997

---

[4]See, for example, Munnell (1990) and Holtz-Eakin (1993) who construct their own state series on capital accumulation.

[5]Because the data are first differenced and lagged one period, we lose two years of data.

increased per-capita income in 1997 by 4.5 percent, or $617 ($806 in $1998). Considering the size of the U.S. population, according to these estimates, the decline in energy intensity made a significant contribution to aggregate welfare over this period. Table A.4 also presents 95 percent confidence intervals around the predicted effect of energy intensity on GSP.[6] Note that this interval widens as we deviate further from the mean value of *Ind. EI* and *Com. EI* (27.56 and 5.28). In 1997, the 95 percent confidence interval lies between $21,738 and $21,753.

Results for Minnesota

The energy intensity coefficients estimated previously represent average effects over the 48 states in the analysis. It is entirely plausible that the effect of energy intensity on economic growth in Minnesota deviates from this average. Unfortunately, we do not have sufficient data to produce these coefficients separately for Minnesota. One approach, then, is simply to apply the energy intensity coefficients estimated for the entire sample to data from Minnesota.

The first three columns in Table A.5 list the mean values of *Ind. EI*, *Com. EI*, and per-capita GSP for Minnesota. As in Table A.4, the fourth column estimates what per-capita income would have been had there been no change in energy intensity between 1977 and 1997 assuming energy intensity has the same effect in Minnesota as it does on average in the other states in our sample. Actual per-capita GSP in Minnesota in 1997 was $24,657. Had there been no change in energy intensity, the model predicts per-capita GSP in 1997 would have been $23,966. By this estimate, the decline in industrial and commercial energy intensity between 1977 and 1997 increased per-capita income in 1997 in Minnesota by 2.9 percent, or $691 ($903 in $1998). Again, since the change in energy intensity in Minnesota deviates from the average change in the entire sample used to calculate $\hat{\alpha}_1$, we generate 95 percent confidence intervals around the predicted effect of energy intensity on GSP as we did in Table A.4. These bounds are presented in columns five and six of Table A.5. These estimates imply that the decline in energy intensity in Minnesota increased per-capita income by between $679 and $703 in 1997.

A second approach is to group states with similar characteristics together and estimate the model separately for each group. The coefficient estimates then presumably reflect the unique circumstances of those states. We experiment with three different categorizations that divide the sample into quartiles based on

---

[6]We approximate this interval as $\hat{y}_j \pm 2\left[\hat{\sigma}X_j(X'X)^{-1}X_j'\right]$.

industrial intensity (i.e., percentage of GSP accounted for by industrial output), industrial energy prices, and climate. We also divide states into those with no, weak, and strong building codes and by DOE region (10 regions).[7] The trouble with this approach, of course, is that by dividing the sample into groups, our coefficient estimates are derived from substantially smaller samples and so are generally less precisely estimated. Also, it is possible that by grouping states in one dimension, we may also group them by some other unknown dimension that could have unpredictable effects on the coefficient estimates.

Table A.6 presents the industrial and commercial energy intensity coefficients for the group of states in which Minnesota falls for each of these five categorizations.[8] The only estimates that seem to tell a consistent story are those based on industrial intensity. We would expect that changes in industrial energy intensity would have less of an effect on GSP in states with relatively low industrial intensity. This is indeed what we see in the data. States in the first quartile of industrial intensity, like Minnesota, have a relatively small and imprecisely estimated coefficient on *Ind. EI* and relatively large coefficient on *Com. EI*. This is reversed in states in the fourth quartile of industrial intensity (not shown)—they have a relatively large coefficient on *Ind. EI* and relatively small coefficient on *Com. EI*. The other categorizations do not yield any discernible pattern in the coefficient estimates.

Table A.7 assumes that the coefficient estimates generated by states of similar industrial intensity are representative of the effect of industrial and commercial energy intensity on GSP in Minnesota. By these estimates, the decline in industrial and commercial energy intensity between 1977 and 1997 increased per-capita income in 1997 in Minnesota by 2.6 percent, or roughly $630 ($823 in $1998). The 95 percent confidence interval for this estimate lies between $607 and $654 in 1997.

The Value of Energy Intensity to the Minnesota Economy

To estimate the value of improvements in energy intensity to the Minnesota economy, we start with the expression used in the regression Eq. (A.2), rewritten as:

---

[7] See Ortiz and Bernstein (1999) for a listing of states by type of building code.

[8] Minnesota is in a quartile of states characterized by moderately high industrial intensity, severe climate, and moderately high industrial energy prices. Minnesota is also among states with moderate building codes.

$$\Delta_t \ln GSP_t = \alpha'_t + \Delta_{t-1} \ln EI_{ind}\alpha_{ind} + \Delta_{t-1} \ln EI_{comm}\alpha_{com}$$

where GSP_t is the gross state product, α'_t is the growth rate of state product in the year t due to all causes except changes in energy intensity, EI_{ind} and EI_{comm} are the industrial and commercial energy intensities, respectively, and α_{ind} and α_{comm} are the coefficients relating changes in energy intensity to changes in the rate of growth of state product.

For the period 1977 to 1997, we have data on the gross state product and the industrial and commercial energy intensities. Using values of the coefficients α_{ind} and α_{comm} obtained from the regression analysis, we can calculate, α'_t, the growth due to factors other than changes in energy intensity. We can then estimate what the state gross product would have been if energy intensity had not improved from 1977 through 1997, by writing

$$\Delta_t \ln GSP'_t = \alpha'_t$$

where the estimate of what gross product would have been without energy intensity improvements depends on our estimates of the impact of energy intensity, as represented by the coefficients α_{ind} and α_{comm}.

The value of the changes in energy intensity that did occur, measured in terms of impacts on state gross product, are thus given in each year t by

$$\text{Value of changes in energy intensity}_t = GSP_t - GSP'_t$$

This estimate depends on our estimates of the coefficients α_{ind} and α_{comm}. Since there is uncertainty in these estimates, we calculate a range of estimates for the value of changes in energy intensity corresponding to our range of estimates for the coefficients.

We can similarly estimate the value of improvements in energy intensity by making forecasts of future growth in gross state product and future trends in energy intensity. Forecasts of each of these factors are available from a variety of sources, but the one thing we know for certain about forecasts is that they are generally wrong. Rather than use a single forecast, we will thus use past trends to create an ensemble of forecasts and calculate the value of changes in energy intensity across this ensemble.[9]

---

[9] The American Heritage dictionary defines ensemble as a unit or group of complementary parts that contribute to a single effect. Our use of the term here is meant to signify that a single forecast is much less valuable than a range of scenarios employed toward a common purpose.

To calculate an ensemble of future growth rates of gross state product due to factors other than changes in energy intensity, we estimate future values of α_t' from its past trends. This growth rate has waxed and waned between 1977 and 1997, with recessions in the early 1980s and 1990s, interspersed with periods of rapid growth. We calculate high, low, and medium estimates for α_t' of 3.24 percent, 2.41 percent, and 1.17 percent by calculating the average growth rates over the periods 1987 to 1997, 1977 to 1997, and 1977 to 1987.

Similarly, we calculate an ensemble of scenarios of future trends in energy intensity, as shown in Figure 3.2, by projecting the average rate of change over that observed from 1977 to 1997, 1977 to 1987, and offer that growth could reverse itself with respect to the rate it grew from 1977 to 1997.

For each combination of forecasted energy intensity trends, state gross product due to factors other than changes in energy intensity, and estimates of the impacts of changes in energy intensity, we can then estimate the future value of the energy intensity using the same formula we used to estimate the past value.

Figure A.1 shows the U.S. energy intensity for the commercial and industrial sectors and Figure A.2 shows the U.S. energy intensity fixed-effect coefficients relative to 1977 energy intensity.

Tables and Figures

Table A.1

U.S. and Minnesota Industrial and Commercial Energy Intensity
(10^3 Btus/1982$): 1977–1997

Year	United States Industrial	United States Commercial	Minnesota Industrial	Minnesota Commercial
1977	30.78	5.84	23.12	4.86
1978	29.57	5.73	23.78	5.13
1979	30.59	5.79	24.02	4.38
1980	31.14	5.92	23.18	4.53
1981	28.97	5.83	21.90	4.69
1982	27.19	5.74	21.90	5.07
1983	26.90	5.36	22.17	4.88
1984	25.95	5.12	19.12	4.71
1985	24.80	4.74	18.87	4.45
1986	23.81	4.37	18.50	3.87
1987	23.82	4.28	18.17	3.56
1988	23.31	4.23	18.89	3.82
1989	24.01	4.22	19.09	3.79
1990	24.87	4.15	20.86	3.75
1991	25.67	4.09	22.51	3.65
1992	26.15	3.84	21.75	3.24
1993	25.66	3.80	23.30	3.21
1994	24.54	3.68	21.52	3.09
1995	24.16	3.68	22.64	3.18
1996	24.31	3.67	21.83	3.23
1997	23.32	3.55	21.99	2.92

Table A.2

The Determinants of Industrial and Commercial Energy Intensity

	Industrial EI Coef.	Industrial EI Std. Err.	Commercial EI Coef.	Commercial EI Std. Err.
P^e	−0.687	0.085	−0.045	0.071
Manufacturing	0.276	0.041	—	—
Mining	0.060	0.170	—	—
New capital	−0.014	0.021	—	—
Building	—	—	−0.152	0.069
Climate	0.242	0.135	0.553	0.110
	Observations: 1,008	R-Squared: 0.933	Observations: 1,008	R-Squared: 0.872

NOTES: All variables are in logs. Regressions include state and time fixed effects. Standard errors are corrected for heteroscedasticity

Table A.3

**The Effect of Energy Intensity on Per-Capita State Economic Growth:
1977–1997**

	Coef.	Std. Err.	95% Confidence Interval
Industrial energy intensity	–0.023	0.006	–0.036 to –0.011
Commercial energy intensity	–0.017	0.008	–0.032 to –0.002
Transportation energy intensity	0.003	0.011	–0.019 to 0.025
Industrial energy prices	–0.010	0.009	–0.027 to 0.006
Commercial energy prices	–0.034	0.008	–0.050 to –0.017
Transportation energy prices	–0.001	0.020	–0.041 to 0.039
Manufacturing GSP	–0.011	0.006	–0.022 to 0.000
Percentage of GSP from mining	0.008	0.003	0.002 to 0.015
New capital expenditures	8.7E–07	4.1E–07	5.9E–08 to 1.7E–06
New building stock	0.186	0.066	0.057 to 0.315
Climate	0.013	0.009	–0.005 to 0.032
Population age 18–64	1.123	0.156	0.816 to 1.430
Population bachelors	–0.003	0.005	–0.014 to 0.007
Percentage GSP from government	–0.329	0.034	–0.396 to –0.263
Percentage GSP from service	–0.741	0.052	–0.844 to –0.638

NOTES: Observations: 912, R-Squared: 0.900. All variables, except *new capital* are in logged first differenced form. See text for variable definitions. Regression controls for state and year fixed effects. Standard errors are corrected for heteroscedasticity across panels.

Table A.4

Predicted Effect of Industrial and Commercial Energy Intensity on State Per-Capita GSP: National Average, 1979–1997

Year	Δ_{t-1} ln *Ind. EI*	Δ_{t-1} ln *Com. EI*	Actual Per-Capita *GSP*	Per-Capita GSP Given No Change in *Ind. EI* or *Com. EI*	Lower-Bound Effect	Upper-Bound Effect
1979	−0.065	−0.023	13,811	13,773	13,760	13,786
1980	0.029	0.003	13,200	13,103	13,097	13,108
1981	0.013	0.026	13,450	13,321	13,315	13,327
1982	−0.067	−0.034	13,299	13,162	13,148	13,175
1983	−0.023	0.007	13,794	13,685	13,681	13,689
1984	−0.006	−0.058	14,988	14,820	14,808	14,832
1985	−0.042	−0.024	15,721	15,502	15,492	15,512
1986	−0.025	−0.067	16,492	16,227	16,210	16,243
1987	−0.030	−0.077	17,186	16,843	16,823	16,863
1988	−0.011	−0.020	18,012	17,606	17,600	17,612
1989	−0.012	0.002	18,072	17,665	17,663	17,668
1990	0.023	−0.002	18,032	17,635	17,630	17,640
1991	0.021	−0.017	18,140	17,763	17,757	17,770
1992	0.032	−0.019	18,723	18,354	18,346	18,363
1993	0.022	−0.075	19,287	18,896	18,875	18,917
1994	−0.017	−0.010	20,279	19,847	19,842	19,852
1995	−0.053	−0.029	20,823	20,331	20,314	20,347
1996	−0.022	−0.013	21,271	20,733	20,726	20,740
1997	−0.021	0.018	22,363	21,746	21,738	21,753

NOTES: Estimates assume a constant marginal effect of *Ind. EI* of −0.022 and *Com. EI* of −0.045 on GSP growth. See text for derivation of lower- and upper-bound effects. All amounts are in 1982$.

Table A.5

Predicted Effect of Industrial and Commercial Energy Intensity on Per-Capita GSP: Minnesota, 1979–1997

Year	Δ_{t-1} ln *Ind. EI*	Δ_{t-1} ln *Com. EI*	Actual Per-Capita GSP	Per-Capita GSP Given No Change in *Ind. EI* or *Com. EI*	Lower-Bound Effect	Upper-Bound Effect
1979	−0.063	−0.036	14,761	14,784	14,771	14,797
1980	−0.146	−0.150	13,860	13,816	13,781	13,851
1981	−0.135	0.049	13,827	13,779	13,770	13,789
1982	0.094	−0.104	13,656	13,598	13,586	13,610
1983	−0.080	0.042	14,399	14,336	14,320	14,352
1984	−0.006	−0.199	16,205	16,025	16,017	16,034
1985	−0.061	−0.067	16,981	16,709	16,677	16,741
1986	−0.057	−0.081	17,939	17,606	17,591	17,621
1987	−0.104	−0.064	18,800	18,381	18,343	18,418
1988	−0.089	−0.068	19,412	18,936	18,912	18,960
1989	−0.135	−0.032	19,511	19,072	19,049	19,094
1990	0.111	0.057	19,240	18,808	18,804	18,811
1991	0.242	−0.002	19,275	18,877	18,855	18,898
1992	−0.022	0.033	20,307	19,886	19,867	19,906
1993	0.125	−0.044	20,487	20,006	19,968	20,043
1994	0.086	−0.061	21,811	21,287	21,270	21,305
1995	−0.104	−0.009	22,384	21,786	21,761	21,811
1996	0.050	−0.031	23,184	22,587	22,570	22,604
1997	0.001	−0.011	24,657	23,966	23,954	23,978

NOTES: Baseline estimates assume a constant marginal effect of *Ind. EI* of −0.022 and *Com. EI* of −0.045 on GSP growth. See text for derivation of lower- and upper-bound effects. All amounts are in 1982$.

Table A.6

The Effect of Industrial and Commercial Energy Intensity on Minnesota's Rate of Economic Growth: Sensitivity Analysis

Group	*Ind. EI* Coef.	*Ind. EI* Std. Err.	*Com. EI* Coef.	*Com. EI* Std. Err.
Moderately high industrial intensity	−0.017	0.013	−0.012	0.011
Moderately high industrial energy prices	−0.016	0.013	−0.020	0.010
Severe climate	−0.019	0.010	−0.023	0.015
Moderate building codes	−0.030	0.009	−0.024	0.008
DOE region	−0.275	0.013	−0.056	0.019

NOTES: Regressions control for all covariates listed in Table A.3. See text for explanation of groupings. Standard errors are corrected for heteroscedasticity across panels.

Table A.7

Predicted Effect of Industrial and Commercial Energy Intensity on Minnesota
Per-Capita GSP: Alternative Coefficient Estimates

Year	Δ_{t-1} ln *Ind. EI*	Δ_{t-1} ln *Com. EI*	Actual Per-Capita GSP	Per-Capita GSP Given No Change in *Ind. EI* or *Com. EI*	Lower-Bound Effect	Upper-Bound Effect
1979	−0.063	−0.036	14,761	14,777	14,757	14,797
1980	−0.146	−0.150	13,860	13,821	13,769	13,874
1981	−0.135	0.049	13,827	13,785	13,769	13,802
1982	0.094	−0.104	13,656	13,606	13,583	13,628
1983	−0.080	0.042	14,399	14,339	14,315	14,363
1984	−0.006	−0.199	16,205	16,030	16,017	16,044
1985	−0.061	−0.067	16,981	16,732	16,670	16,794
1986	−0.057	−0.081	17,939	17,636	17,614	17,658
1987	−0.104	−0.064	18,800	18,428	18,372	18,483
1988	−0.089	−0.068	19,412	18,995	18,959	19,030
1989	−0.135	−0.032	19,511	19,119	19,084	19,154
1990	0.111	0.057	19,240	18,854	18,848	18,860
1991	0.242	−0.002	19,275	18,915	18,871	18,958
1992	−0.022	0.033	20,307	19,920	19,881	19,958
1993	0.125	−0.044	20,487	20,056	20,000	20,113
1994	0.086	−0.061	21,811	21,334	21,298	21,370
1995	−0.104	−0.009	22,384	21,848	21,802	21,895
1996	0.050	−0.031	23,184	22,642	22,611	22,673
1997	0.001	−0.011	24,657	24,027	24,003	24,050

NOTES: Baseline estimates assume a constant marginal effect of *Ind. EI* of −0.020 and
Com. EI of −0.054 on GSP growth. See text for derivation of lower- and upper-bound effects.
All amounts are in 1982$.

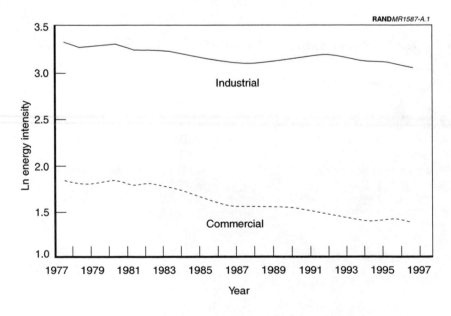

Figure A.1—U.S. Energy Intensity: 1977–1997

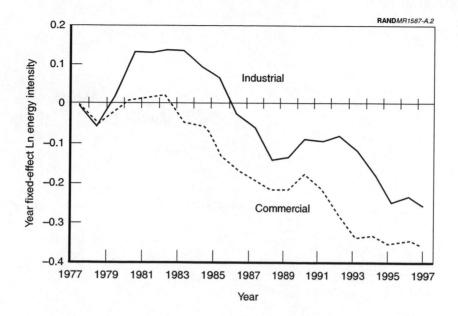

**Figure A.2—U.S. Energy Intensity Fixed-Effect Coefficients Relative to
1977 Energy Intensity**

Bibliography

Baker, D. G., E. L.Kuehnast, and J. A. Zandle. 1985. *Climate of Minnesota: Part XV—Normal Temperatures (1951-1980) and Their Application.* University of Minnesota. www.climate.umn.edu/pdf/climate_of_minnesota/comXV.pdf.

Barro, R. J., and X. Sala-i-Martin. 1995. *Economic Growth.* New York: McGraw-Hill.

BEA. See U.S. Bureau of Economic Analysis.

Berndt, E. R., and D. O. Wood. 1974. "An Economic Interpretation of the Energy-GNP Ratio," in M. S. Macrakis (ed.), *Energy: Demand, Conservation, and Institutional Problems.* Cambridge: MIT Press.

Bernstein, M. A., R. Lempert, D. Loughran, and D. Ortiz. 2000. *The Public Benefit of California's Investment in Energy Efficiency.* MR-1212.0-CEC. Santa Monica, Calif.: RAND.

Berry, Linda G., and Marylyn A. Brown. 1996. "Energy-Efficiency Improvements and Remaining Opportunities in the DOE Low-Income Weatherization Program." *1996 ACEEE Summer Study on Energy Efficiency in Buildings,* Washington, D.C.: American Council for an Energy Efficient Economy.

Berry, Linda G., Marylyn A. Brown, and Laurence F. Kinney. 1997. *Progress Report of the National Weatherization Assistance Program.* ORNL/CON-450. Oak Ridge, Tenn.: Oak Ridge National Laboratory, Department of Energy.

Brown, Marylyn A., Linda G. Berry, and Laurence F. Kinney. 1994. *Weatherization Works: Final Report of the National Weatherization Evaluation.* ORNL/CON-395. Oak Ridge, Tenn.: Oak Ridge National Laboratory.

Census. See U.S. Census Bureau.

Chandrasekar, G., Young-Doo Wang, John Byrne, and Kyunghee Ham. 1994. "Utility Sponsored Low-Income Weatherization as a DSM option." *1994 ACEEE Summer Study on Energy Efficiency in Buildings,* Washington, D.C.: American Council for an Energy Efficient Economy.

Colton, Roger D. 1994. *The Other Part of the Year: Low-Income Households and Their Need for Cooling. A State-by-State Analysis of Low-Income Summer Electric Bills.* Belmont, Mass.: Fisher, Sheehan & Colton.

Crain, W. M., and K. J. Lee. 1999. "Economic Growth Regressions for the American States: A Sensitivity Analysis." *Economic Inquiry,* 37(2): 242–57.

Denison, E. F. 1962. *The Sources of Economic Growth in the United States and the Alternatives Before Us.* New York: Committee for Economic Development.

DHHS. See U.S. Department of Health and Human Services.

DOE. See U.S. Department of Energy.

Dowlatabadi, H. and M. A. Oravetz. 1997. "U.S. Long-Term Energy Intensity: Backcast & Projection." Unpublished working paper. Pittsburgh, Pa.: Department of Engineering and Public Policy, Carnegie Mellon University.

EIA. See U.S. Department of Energy, Energy Information Administration.

Electric Power Research Institute (EPRI). *Project 1940-25 Final Report: Demand Side Management Glossary.* TR101158. Palo Alto, Calif.

EPA. See U.S. Environmental Protection Agency.

Eto, J. 1996. *The Past, Present, and Future of U.S. Utility Demand-Side Management Programs.* LBNL-39931. Berkeley, Calif.: Lawrence Berkeley National Laboratory. December.

Eto, J., S. Kito, L. Shown, and R. Sonnenblick. 1995. *Where Did the Money Go? The Cost and Performance of the Largest Commercial Sector DSM Programs.* LBL-38201. Berkeley, Calif.: Lawrence Berkeley National Laboratory. December.

F. W. Dodge and Co. 1999. http://fwdodge.construction.com; construction data were contracted from them.

Fox-Penner, Peter. 1998. *Electric Utility Restructuring: A Guide to the Competitive Era.* Vienna, Va.: Public Utilities Reports, Inc.

Golove, W. H., and J. H. Eto. 1996. *Market Barriers to Energy Efficiency: A Critical Reappraisal of the Rationale for Public Policies to Promote Energy Efficiency.* LBL-38059. Berkeley, Calif. Lawrence Berkeley National Laboratory. March.

Greene, W. H. 1993. *Econometric Analysis,* 2nd Edition. New York: Macmillan Publishing Company.

Griliches, Z. 1998. *R&D and Productivity: The Econometric Evidence.* Chicago: University of Chicago Press.

Griliches, Z., and J. Mairesse. 1995. *Production Functions: The Search for Identification.* NBER Working Paper #5067. Cambridge, Mass.: NBER.

Holtz-Eakin, D. 1993. "Solow and the States: Capital Accumulation, Productivity, and Economic Growth." *National Tax Journal,* 46(4): 425–39.

Howat, John, and Jerrold Oppenheim. 1999. *Analysis of Low-Income Benefits in Determining Cost-Effectiveness of Energy Efficiency Programs.* Washington, D.C.: National Consumer Law Center.

Jorgenson, D. W., F. M. Gollop, and B. M Fraumeni. 1987. *Productivity and U.S. Economic Growth.* Cambridge, Mass.: Harvard University Press.

Jorgenson, D. W., and Z. Griliches. 1967. "The Explanation of Productivity Change." *Review of Economics and Statistics,* 34(3): 249–83.

Kennedy, P. 1998. *A Guide to Econometrics,* 4th Edition. Cambridge, Mass.: MIT Press.

MDOC. See Minnesota Department of Commerce.

Megdal, Lori M., and Melissa Piper. 1994. "Finding Methods to Estimate Social Benefits of Low-Income Energy Efficiency Programs." *1994 ACEEE Summer Study on Energy Efficiency in Buildings,* Washington, D.C.: American Council for an Energy Efficient Economy.

Minnesota State Demographic Center (MSDC). 1998. *Faces of the Future: Minnesota County Population Projections 1995-2025.*

Moezzi, Mithra. 1999. *The Predicament of Efficiency.* Berkeley, Calif.: Lawrence Berkeley National Laboratory. Self-published by the author.

Munnell, A. H. 1990. "How Does Public Infrastructure Affect Regional Economic Performance?" *New England Economic Review,* September/October, 11–32.

Nadel, S., T. Kubo, and H. Geller. 2000. *State Scorecard on Utility Energy Efficiency Programs.* Washington, D.C.: American Council for an Energy Efficient Economy. April.

National Center for Appropriate Technology (NCAT). 2001a. *Low Income Home Energy Assistance Program FY 2001 State Allotments Funding Tables.* www.ncat.org/liheap/tables/01-14im4.xls.

_____. 2001b. 1999–2000. *State-by-State Supplements to Energy Assistance and Energy Efficiency.* www.ncat.org/liheap/tables/stsupup2.htm.

National Consumer Law Center (NCLC). 1995. *Energy and the Poor: The Crisis Continues.* Washington, D.C.

NCLC. See National Consumer Law Center.

NERC. See North American Electric Reliability Council.

North American Electric Reliability Council (NERC). 1999. *1999 Summer Assessment, Reliability of Bulk Electricity Supply in North America.* June.

_____. 2000. *Reliability Assessment 2000–2009. The Reliability of Bulk Electric Systems in North America.* October. ftp://www.nerc.com/pub/sys/all_updl/docs/pubs/2000ras.pdf

Olds, Katy. 1996. *Low-Income Working Group Report.* Sacramento: California/Nevada Community Action Association.

Ortiz, D. S., and M. A. Bernstein. 1999. *Measures of Residential Energy Consumption and Their Relationships to DOE Policy.* MR-1105.0-DOE. Santa Monica, Calif.: RAND. November.

Pye, Miriam. 1996. *Energy Efficiency Programs for Low-Income Households: Successful Approaches for a Competitive Environment.* Washington, D.C.: American Council for an Energy Efficient Economy.

Rosenberg, N. 1983. "The Effects of Energy Supply Characteristics on Technology and Economic Growth," in S. H. Schurr, S. Sonenblum, and D. O. Wood (eds.), *Energy, Productivity, and Economic Growth.* Cambridge, Mass.: Oelgeschlager, Gunn & Hain.

Schurr, S. H. 1983. "Energy Efficiency and Economic Efficiency: An Historical Perspective," in S. H. Schurr, S. Sonenblum, and D. O Wood (eds.), *Energy, Productivity, and Economic Growth.* Cambridge, Mass: Oelgeschlager, Gunn & Hain.

Schurr, S. H., and B. C. Netschert. 1960. *Energy in the American Economy: 1850–1975.* Baltimore, Md.: The Johns Hopkins Press.

Solow, J. L. 1987. "The Capital-Energy Complementarity Debate Revisited." *American Economic Review,* 77(4): 605–14.

Solow, R. M. 1957. "Technical Change and the Aggregate Production Function." *Review of Economics and Statistics,* 39(3): 312–20.

State of Minnesota, Department of Commerce (MDOC). 2001. *Minnesota Energy Planning Report 2001.* www.commerce.state.mn.us/pages/Energy/MainEnergyPolicy.htm.

U.S. Bureau of Economic Analysis (BEA). 1999.

U.S. Census Bureau (Census). 1999. *American Housing Survey.* www.census.gov/hhes/www/housing/ahs/appa.html.

U.S. Department of Energy (DOE). 1997. *Progress Report of the National Weatherization Assistance Program.* Oak Ridge, Tenn.: Oak Ridge National Laboratory, Tennessee.

_____. 2001. *Minnesota Energy Data.* www.eia.doe.gov/emeu/states/main_ma.html

U.S. Department of Energy, Energy Information Administration (EIA). 1999a. *State Energy Data Report, 1997.* DOE/EIA-0214(97). Washington, D.C.: U.S. Government Printing Office. September.

_____. 1999b. *A Look at Residential Energy Consumption in 1997.* DOE/EIA-0632(97). Washington, D.C.: U.S. Government Printing Office. November.

_____. 1998a. *State Energy Price and Expenditure Report, 1995.* DOE/EIA-0376(95). Washington, D.C.: U.S. Government Printing Office. August.

_____. 1998b. *A Look at Commercial Buildings in 1995: Characteristics, Energy Consumption, and Energy Expenditures.* DOE/EIA-0625(95). Washington, D.C.: U.S. Government Printing Office. October.

_____. 1995a. *Measuring Energy Efficiency in the United States' Economy: A Beginning.* DOE/EIA-0555(95)/2. Washington, D.C.: U.S. Government Printing Office. October.

_____. 1995b. *Household Energy Consumption and Expenditures 1993 Supplement: State-by-State Data.* Washington, D.C.: U.S. Government Printing Office.

U.S. Department of Energy, Office of Building Technology, State and Community Programs. 2001. *DOE Status of Energy Codes.* www.eren. doe.gov/buildings/codes_standards/buildings/states/states_list.html.

U.S. Department of Health and Human Services (DHHS). 1999. Number of LIHEAP Households Assisted in FFY 2000, by state Draft Tabulations as of February 2002. www.acf.dhhs.gov/programs/liheap/fy95hhs.htm

U.S. Environmental Protection Agency, Office of Air Quality Planning and Standards (EPA). 2001. *Office of Air and Radiation.* www.epa.gov/agweb.

_____. 2000. *Emissions & Generation Resource Integrated Database (E-GRID).* Washington, D.C.: www.epa.gov/airmarkets/egrid/.

MR-1587-EF